TheSkinnyOn™

COLLEGE **SUCCESS**

JIM RANDEL AND **CAROL RANDEL**

The SkinnyOn™ College Success
COLLEGE & CAREER

TABLE OF CONTENTS

1 MAKING THE TRANSITION TO COLLEGE

I AM IN CHARGE OF MY OWN SUCCESS

hello...

You're on your own. You may still live at home; you may get daily phone calls from your parents to your dorm, but your education is now in your hands. There is even a federal privacy law (FERPA) prohibiting colleges from communicating with your parents about your progress unless you give your permission. It is a startling thought that there is no one to stop you from failing now. On the other hand, your success is all yours, too. Being a successful student is simpler than you might think. Follow these basic principles:

- BE THERE

- 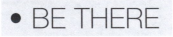 DO THE WORK

- GET HELP

- PLAN

- THINK

There it is—**college success in a nutshell**. All the pages that follow fall under one of the above categories. The extra benefit of taking responsibility for mastering these principles is that they will also lead to success in life.

BE THERE

Successful students go to class. It is the first and most simple rule for learning and getting good grades.

New college students are often unpleasantly surprised to discover that material presented in class is not a duplication of material in a textbook or handout. If you miss the class, you miss essential information. Even if you get notes from another student (which you should if you are absent), it is not the same as being there. Would you rather go to a movie or have your friend summarize it for you? There are attendance policies in all classes, and missing a certain percentage of class for any reason will usually result in a failing grade.

Being there **in body**, however, is not enough.

You must be an active listener and participant in order to get the most out of a class. A student who lets his or her focus wander to the scene outside the window may as well be absent.

Successful Students...

- Are prepared for class with pen, paper, books, and class material

- Are on time (professors get extremely annoyed at students who walk in after class has started)

- Pay attention

- Take notes

- Ask and answer questions

In college, **assignments** are an essential part of the course.

You're not in class all day, but you are expected to take on your own part of the learning by doing the assignments. Grades are largely based on completed assignments and exams that require semester-long study, not cramming.

Unlike in high school, assignments in college are not necessarily collected every day. Often, due dates are days or weeks in the future, and no one will be making sure that you are keeping up with the reading, or writing reflection pieces in your journal, or doing the research for your paper.

The ways you will know that you have not kept up are when you fail a test, get an F on a paper, or get hopelessly lost as new concepts are added to concepts you never mastered in the first place.

Missed assignments will be reflected in your grade. They will also be reflected in how well you learn and remember the material. Keep in mind, college is for you. There is no point in being there if you are not learning anything.

College courses can be difficult. When students find the work very challenging, they tend to skip classes, stop handing in work, drop courses, or even leave school.

You can avoid embarking on the road toward failure by **seeking help at the first sign of trouble**.

All instructors have office hours. These are provided so students can go to their teachers for extra help when needed. Often, various departments provide small-group sessions such as recitations or math labs to practice concepts and skills.

Colleges have many services available that provide academic support for students. There are tutoring and writing centers that provide peer support and/or professional tutors to assist students in understanding the material and effectively writing essays and papers. Often, just having the material explained by someone with a different perspective is helpful. And one-on-one instruction is always a good way to increase comprehension.

There are many kinds of programs offered, often supported by federal grants, to help students succeed. The student handbook and your school's financial aid department will have a list of such services.

Use your planner to account for how you will spend your time.

There are some commitments that are fixed, such as class and work hours. Most other activities are discretionary, though essential, and you must decide when and for how long you will do them. By scheduling time for study, exercise, social activities, meals, chores and sleep, you will go a long way toward ensuring your success.

THINK

You will hear a lot about using your critical-thinking skills in college. There is almost no need for the adjective "critical"—**just think**.

Time to come off of cruise control and engage your education. Start questioning all your old assumptions, judgments, and evaluations. Start creating new associations, connections, and conclusions.

If you leave college thinking the same thoughts you did when you entered, you have wasted several years of your life.

There is a reason you are taking all these courses you have never studied before. The reason is not to please your parents, the college administration, or even to enter some career. The real reason to learn is to grow.

What is This Thing Called **Syllabus**?

They'll hand you one of these in every class on the first day. You will be tempted to stuff it in your book bag—and promptly lose it. Don't. It is your consumer protection plan, your instruction manual, your contacts list.

Your syllabus tells you:

- What the course is about
- The goal, objectives, and/or learning outcomes of the course
- What book(s) you will be using
- Class policies
- How to reach your instructor (e-mail address, phone number, office number)
- Your instructor's office hours

A course outline is often attached to the syllabus, showing the subject of each class meeting and the assignments for the semester.

Instructors do not look kindly on students who protest that they don't know how to reach a professor, or don't know what the assignment is, when it was on the syllabus.

Hang on to your syllabus. Put it in your class notebook for easy reference.

Along with your syllabus, many instructors will list behavioral expectations for their class such as attendance and tardy policies. Reading these expectations carefully will keep your instructor happy. One of the expectations will be to turn off all cell phones.

There is no quicker way to make a professor **angry** than by texting during class…

…except by texting during a test—which brings up academic honesty/dishonesty policies. There are many ways to cheat in the age of technology. Your professor knows them all and has little patience for academic dishonesty. That includes cheating on tests, collaborating on assignments when not directed to do so, using work from one class for another class without permission, and using outside sources, including sources from the Internet, without citation (plagiarism).

Colleges have policies to deal with academic dishonesty, and they enforce them. They usually contain escalating consequences for each offense and end with expulsion.

The bottom line is: Cheating makes no sense. It's your education—by taking shortcuts you are wasting your opportunities to learn.

Anyway, is being a cheater one of your goals for success in your future?

From the first day of classes you will be thrown in with all sorts of students, faculty, and staff. Unlike in high school, these people have no preconceived notion of who you are! This can be a wonderfully freeing feeling. **You can reinvent yourself.**

Were you the kid in high school who never spoke up in class? Even if you wanted to change your ways and start contributing, you may have resisted the impulse for fear that those who have known you for years would laugh at you. From the first day of class in your new environment, you can be that student who raises a hand when a question is asked.

The flip side of all this newness is that you can feel lonely or isolated—a stranger in a strange place. It is possible to get through an entire semester without knowing the names of the other students in your class. It's even possible to leave a class without knowing your professor's name (especially if you lost the syllabus that included his/her name and contact information). It is up to you to make connections with other people at school—and it's a good idea.

I'M **outgoing!**

I'M a questioning **machine!**

YEP! That's **me**!

Learn his or her **name**!

HELLO, I'm **Mr.**
_____!

- So that you can contact him/her for help. (School e-mail addresses are often based on names.)

- So that you can call him/her by name (professors get a warm and fuzzy feeling when called by name).

- So that you can get in touch with that professor in later years. When you need a college instructor's recommendation on an application for a job or graduate school, it's a sad shock to discover that there is no teacher you can turn to because none of them knew you. You never made a connection!

Many college professors want their students to be successful and will spend time to help them—**but only if the student asks**! The key idea here is that you must be the one to reach out. Go to your professor during office hours, ask questions, and make yourself known. Instructors are human (really) and will give the benefit of the doubt when it comes to grading students whom they see as sincerely interested and willing to make the effort to succeed in their classes.

CONNECT WITH OTHER STUDENTS

College is a place to form new relationships. Many people make lifelong friendships in college.

Many people find that future career success is enhanced by the networks they created with fellow students in college. Actually, socializing with people who were not raised in your hometown is one of the most valuable learning experiences college has to offer.

Making connections to other students also enhances your academic success.

Unlike in high school, college students are often encouraged to work with other students by forming study groups, which are a good way to learn material. Explaining concepts that you understand to students who are having trouble with them is a great way to reinforce your own comprehension. Working through material that you find difficult with students who have grasped the concepts is a good way to learn. Reviewing for exams with other students in the class is more fun, and ensures that you are making time to study, which will help you be successful in the course.

At the very least, get contact information from one student in each of your classes so you can get notes and find out what happened if you miss a class.

Boring! You have enough new books to tackle without having to waste time reading your student handbook, right?

Surprisingly, the handbook is full of useful information that may take months for you to discover on your own, or that you might never discover at all. Most handbooks are posted online so that you can refer to them at any time. Take the opportunity to check out the handbook at the beginning of your first semester.

There are things that you **need to know**, such as:

> Policies and procedures, including any penalties involved in breaking them

> Reference guide to services, clubs, activities, and academic advisors

> Locations of the career center, fitness facilities, financial aid office, campus employment office, the lost and found, and other areas

> Special programs and available scholarships

> Codes of conduct

> Ways to resolve complaints or file grievances

> Names of the president, deans, and other important administration, faculty, and staff

2 GOAL-SETTING

Psychologists distinguish between **external** values and **intrinsic** values.

External values are those dictated by others—society in general: the obtaining of money, power, respect, and fame. Internal values are more about you:

What personal beliefs are fundamental to who and what you are?

Studies have shown that when people put all of their energy toward obtaining goals founded on external values rather than on internal beliefs, the likelihood of goal achievement decreases. Yes, many of us want money, fame, power, and respect. But the pursuit of these goals must align with our most fundamental beliefs, or the probability of success is low.

> "People who seek a job purely on the basis of money rarely find either a satisfying job or the money they desire."
>
> ANONYMOUS

In other words, to be as **successful** as possible in achieving your dreams and goals, you cannot **divorce** your goals from your most basic values.

Thinking about how **you** define **"success"** will tell you a lot about yourself.

If you were to fast-forward twenty years, what would you want your life to look like? **That is how you define "success."**

There is no right and wrong answer about how you define success. There is nothing wrong with wanting material success. What's more, material and spiritual success are not mutually exclusive.

Do not be influenced by what you think others expect of you. Decide what success will be for you. Once you do that, you can then work backwards in crafting a plan from getting where you are today … to where you eventually hope to be.

"The great successful people of the world have used their imagination... they think ahead and create their mental picture in all its details, filling in here, adding a little there, altering this a bit and that a bit, but steadily building—steadily building."

ROBERT COLLIER, AMERICAN AUTHOR

Goal achievement is, to some degree, about **visualization**—about the ability to project an image several years ahead to see what and how you are living **"into the future."**

One of the great stories of achievement lore is that of Jim Carrey, who came to Hollywood from his native Canada with little more than a dream. He believed that somehow, someway, he would make it as a movie star.

And he visualized his success. In fact, to put real specificity to the picture, soon after arriving in Hollywood he wrote himself a check for $10,000,000 (even though his account at the time had perhaps $1,000) and postdated it five years.

As he wrote the check, he **visualized** himself going into a bank and cashing the check.

And here is the fun part. Because of movies like Ace Ventura: Pet Detective and others, Carrey was actually able to cash that check within five years—perhaps in large part because he was able to visualize his success and live every moment of every day working toward his picture-perfect day (cashing the check).

WHAT IS A GOAL?

Webster's Dictionary defines **"goal"** as:

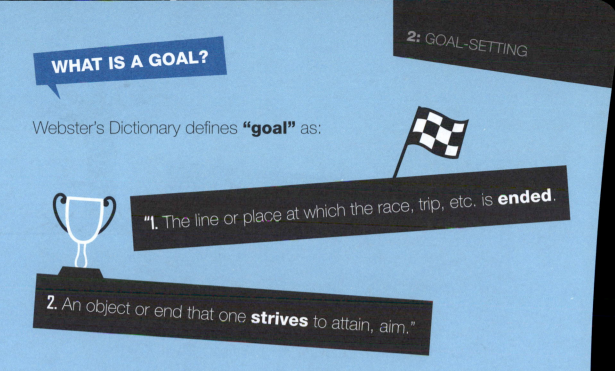

"1. The line or place at which the race, trip, etc. is **ended**.

2. An object or end that one **strives** to attain, aim."

Although the second definition seems more like what we are discussing, the first definition is also important because it reminds us that a goal should be finite. **In other words, there should be an end date in mind.**

In order to create effective goals you need to be specific about what you are going to accomplish and by when.

Some people set vague goals (e.g., "to do better in school next semester"). Goals like that never seem to work. What does "better" actually mean?

A goal should be precise (e.g., "to improve my GPA to _____").

Similarly, a goal should have an end date (e.g., "by no later than the end of May, I will have _____").

If you want to maximize the probability of achieving your goals, you need to be precise as to exactly what it is you seek to accomplish and by when.

Adding **precision** to the equation helps your mind process what needs to get done by when.

There is no standard definition for a long- or short-term goal.

For purposes of this book, let's think of a short-term goal as an objective that can be achieved within one year, and a long-term goal as everything else.

You should also be careful about what you consider a goal. A goal is something you need to **strive** for over a period of time and that will **challenge you** to some degree.

Distinguish between a "**task**," a "**chore**," or even an "**obligation**." These latter descriptions are more appropriate to items you would put on a daily or weekly To-Do List.

One way to think about tasks and goals:

"Tasks go on To-Do Lists; goals go on Mission Statements."

One other important point: Over time, people's goals change. Every six months or so, at least for your long-term goals, find a quiet time and space to reflect on them. Perhaps changes are in order. We also suggest writing down your goals—the act of writing imprints a visual image of achievement in your mind.

YOUR GOALS

There are no right and wrong goals. What is **important to you** is all that matters.

When you write your goals, it is a time to **let your mind fly**.

Forget for the moment what is practical, even perhaps what is realistic. Goal-setting is your time to "create"—at least on paper—your dreamscape, the ideal life you would like to live. In order to create effective goals you need to be specific about what you are going to accomplish and by when.

Consider keeping your goals to yourself. No one knows you better than you know yourself. If you open up to others what your long-term goals are, they may have comments that are not conducive to your achievement.

Many successful people (some of whom we presume wrote down their goals) were discouraged from pursuing something important to them by a parent or other person in authority. People like Elvis Presley, Paul McCartney, and Barbra Streisand were all told at one time or another that they should give up music— "what a silly waste of time" they may have been told. **Fortunately, they did not listen!!**

CREATING AN ACTION PLAN

The most important thing to learn about goals is that thinking about them is not enough. Far too many people take the step of identifying their goals … and then just wait for them to happen.

Consider the old adage:

"Nothing great just **happens**."

What that saying means is that if you want something great to happen in your life, you are going to have to **make it happen**! Wishing, hoping, daydreaming, and even writing down goals, all that is nice,

but as Einstein said:

"NOTHING HAPPENS until there is **action.**"

Sooner or later you are going to realize that your life is in your hands, for better or worse. No one is going to come along and create the life you want. So, if you want to achieve your goals, you have to determine what steps are necessary to get from here to there and **start moving**.

Good News: Many people do not know the precise steps to take them to the realization of their goals. BUT, by moving forward, in the **DIRECTION** of their goals, they start to find the path—**or steps**—that takes them where they want to go.

3 TIME MANAGEMENT

"Time management" is an often-used phrase. But, what does it mean?

It refers to the collection of skills, techniques, strategies, and attitudes that allow a person to use time most **effectively**.

For each of us, an hour is 60 minutes or 3,600 seconds. But some people know how to make better use of an hour than others. Those who practice effective time management are more likely to achieve their goals and aspirations.

> "Those who respect time the least are the same people bemoaning that there is not enough time in the day."
>
> ANONYMOUS

Time is a fleeting asset. Simply acknowledging this is a first step toward making better use of your time.

On the other hand, time management is not about trying to maximize the productivity of every hour in your life. Life is a continuing balance between growth and achievement, and relaxation and leisure. Finding the right balance is one of the challenges we face in pursuit of a healthy life. In this chapter, we will help you identify what it is you want to do with the 24-hour gift we call a "day."

TIME JOURNALS

In order to get a better sense of how effective a time manager you may **(or may not)** be, you need to track how you are spending your time. A time journal can help you do that.

"Flying blind is one way of describing people who have no sense of how they are allocating their daily gift—the hours of a day."

ANONYMOUS

A time journal is nothing more than a diary. We suggest that at the end of every day for one week, you enter in increments of 30 minutes what you did in the preceding 24 hours. General categories might be:

1. **Sleep**

2. **Class time**

3. **Class preparation and study**

4. **Phone or text friends**

5. **TV or Internet**

6. **Recreation**

7. **Eating**

8. **Shower, dress for school**

9. **Exercise**

10. **Miscellaneous**

There is no magic to the categories or form of a time journal. The point is for you to see how you are allocating your most precious resource—your time. Preparing a time journal might surprise you. You might find that you are spending more (or less) time on certain activities than you should.

One way to improve your time-management skills is to get the most you can out of every classroom hour. Our advice here is pretty basic: The more energy and curiosity you bring to your class time, the more you will take from it.

Energy comes from getting enough sleep and developing healthy habits, including exercise and healthy eating. The more energy you bring to your class time, the more you will take out of each class. When it comes to time management, some experts say the discussion should not be about time, per se, but rather about energy.

If you want to achieve a lot in life, learn to maximize your energy. One energetic hour is more valuable than spending five hours just "going through the motions."

Most experts state that you need about **2 to 2.5 hours** outside of class for every **one hour** in class. These 2 to 2.5 hours are for tasks such as assignments, reading, studying, and writing papers.

No matter how you slice it, this graph describes school performance for **99% of the student body:**

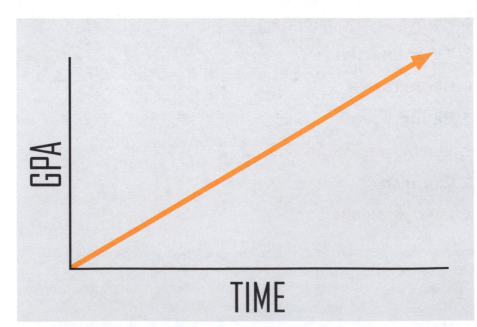

OK, now that you know you need 2 to 2.5 hours of time outside of class for every hour in class, you need to make sure it's feasible for you. So, if you are taking 15 hours of course credits this semester, you need to determine if you have **30** to **40 hours** every week to spend on tasks outside class time.

If you do have those hours available, an equally important question is, do you have the self-discipline to use those hours for schoolwork?

Most students have a lot going on in their lives. A large part of everyone's life is choosing among all the competing alternatives for each minute and hour, but we will get to that.

First, you have to be sure that you have enough space in the week to allocate for class time and outside class time. If you are taking 15 credits, then you need to have about 50 hours available to you per week for a solid performance in school. Do you have that? Refer back to your time journal. What other major obligations do you have? (Job, sports, family, etc.)

OK, other than school, my activities total 125 hours per week. But wait, I need 50 hours for school time … 24 x 7 = 168. UH OH.

Balancing all that you have going on is a constant struggle.

If you want to accomplish your goals you need to find and guard the time you need to make them happen.

There have been several recent studies conducted on top achievers, including athletes, entertainers, and business people. A very small percentage of top performers succeeded through sheer talent, braininess, or athleticism. But most got to where they wanted to be through hours and hours of focused practice, preparation, and persistence.

Presumably, you have some goals for your years in school and for your years after school. Whatever your goals may be, you need to understand and acknowledge the **direct correlation between time invested and goal achievement.**

CHOICES

Now we've come to one of the thorniest topics in this chapter—**the need to make choices**.

The choices you make every day will affect your life and your future. It is not necessarily true that if you do poorly in school, you are destined to be a failure in life. Every person hits his or her stride at different times.

But, if you do not develop the ability to make good choices—now, right now—you may very well fall far short of not only your goals, but of your potential.

Often your decisions will come down to:

1. Doing today **exactly what you feel like doing**,

OR

2. Doing today **what will prepare you for a better life tomorrow**.

The choices you can make today—to do your best in school, to lead a healthy life, to treat others with respect and compassion—will not only prepare you for what comes next, but will also help you develop the habits and routines you will need in the competitive world awaiting you.

> "Successful people do not enjoy doing the things that others do not want to do, but they do them nevertheless."
>
> ALBERT E.N. GRAY

CLEVER, but **not good advice**!

Mark Twain said:

"Never put off to tomorrow what you can put off to the day after tomorrow."

Procrastination is the **enemy** of achievement.

Procrastination is the word we give the myriad of excuses we all have for putting off working at a project, chore, or challenge. Procrastination is just so darn easy.

Success in school and in life will depend upon your ability to take action. As Einstein said, "Nothing happens until something moves." If you want to move forward in life, you will have to defeat the urge to procrastinate.

Procrastination is powerful. We know from the law of inertia that a body at rest will stay at rest unless and until acted upon by an outside force. Inertia is a powerful force. But physics also tells us that a body in motion will stay in motion until acted upon by an outside force. So, once you do get moving, it will be easier to stay moving!

YOU MUST LEARN TO BEAT BACK **INERTIA**

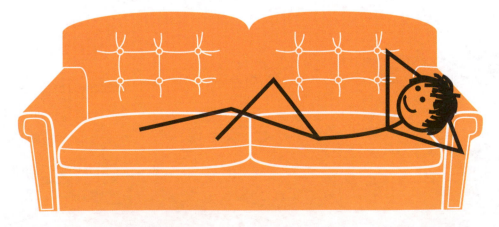

PRIORITIZING

Prioritizing is about making choices between two competing realities:

1. There are only so many hours in the day.

VS.

2. How much time you give to your goals will directly affect your achievement.

We have already discussed choices and making the hard decisions that will allow you to find as much time as possible to devote to your objectives. But, time management is not just about isolating time. It is just as much about using the time you have effectively. **That is what prioritizing is about.**

Not all activities are going to move you closer to your objectives. Some are going to have more of an effect than others. Prioritizing means developing a sequence in all that you have to do.

What should you do first, then second and so on—with the understanding that as the day progresses, things may intervene that will prevent you from getting to everything?

★ Which activities are **important**, not just urgent?

➜ Which activities can be **delayed** and which cannot?

Deciding, every single day, the sequence of what you will do and when is called "prioritizing." And how you prioritize your days' tasks can have an enormous effect on what you actually achieve.

Having the proper amount of time allocated to class time and outside class time is important, of course, but if you do not take advantage of those hours, you are just kidding yourself.

The **#1 determinant** for powerful and effective time management is FOCUS.

Did you ever use a magnifying glass to train the sun's rays on a leaf or piece of paper? When the heat from the sun is concentrated, it can light a fire. That's how to think of focus.

When you train all of your mental capabilities on a task, the heat and power of your brain power is concentrated. The result may be a fire—a kind of spontaneous combustion of creativity, problem-solving and substantive analysis.

As the enemy of action is procrastination, the enemy of focus is distraction. And like procrastination, distractions are so very seductive. You get the picture: you are sitting down to study and your cell phone rings. Or, you get a text message or e-mail ding. Or, someone drops in on you. GAME OVER. Your focus is gone.

If you want to get the most out of every hour, you need to prevent distractions. Shut off your cell phone. Log off the Internet. Turn off the "dings." Put on a baseball cap and pull down the visor. Single-minded focus. That's where it's at.

THE 80-20 RULE

One day in 1906, an Italian economist named Pareto was working in his garden. As usual, he was lovingly caring for all his plants when he got an idea.

"Wow, every season just a few plants produce the great majority of the good vegetables. I wonder what would happen if I spend most of my energy on just the high-producing plants?"

Pareto started focusing most of his energy on his high-producing plants and the results were startling. With no extra effort, the output from his garden grew dramatically and so was born the 80-20 rule.

80% of your results will come from **20%** of your efforts.

Pareto's observation has been applied to many areas:

Salespeople know that 80% of their revenue comes from 20% of their accounts.

Investors know that 80% of their returns come from 20% of their investments.

And so on.

The key is to figure out which activities are contributing the most to the progression toward your goals. **Here's how to apply the 80-20 rule to your own life:**

Describe one of your goals.

_____

_____

Describe five activities you undertake to help you achieve your goal.

1. _____

2. _____

3. _____

4. _____

5. _____

Which of those activities is moving you closer to your goal most quickly?

_____

Try putting an extra amount of your time into that activity, and see what happens.

Effective time management does not mean always being busy.

You see, expending time, in and of itself, is not the route to success. What does lead to success is **effective** time management—using time in a powerful and productive fashion.

Too many people equate being busy with being effective, when in fact one has nothing to do with the other. Keeping busy can be a way for people to convince themselves that they are achieving their goals. But always moving is not the same as moving forward. Busyness is often just tumult—lots of movement and noise without any movement toward your goals.

> "Forget time management. I used to convince myself that I would live by volume ..."
>
> *THE 4-HOUR WORKWEEK*, TIMOTHY FERRISS

Ferriss does not actually mean to forget time management, but forget the idea that being busy is the same as being effective. Reflect on the difference and whether the things that are keeping you busy are actually helping you to achieve your goals.

TECHNIQUES FOR EFFECTIVE TIME USAGE

There are a ton of books on time-management techniques and strategies.

Hey, good news. We have read them all and we are going to summarize them for you.

Pick and choose what you think will work best for you:

1. **Make to-do lists**—no one can remember everything!

2. **Develop a good filing system**—put everything on a particular subject in one place.

3. **Touch just once**—when something comes into your day, whether it's paper or digital, make an immediate decision what to do with it. Don't push it aside to deal with "later" if at all possible.

4. **Learn to discard**—get rid of stuff as soon as you can.

5. **Establish defined times to check e-mails, texts, and phone messages.** Every time you are interrupted from what you are doing, it takes time (after the interruption) to get back into it. Your momentum is broken.

6. **Wear a watch all the time.**

7. **Take action**—when you have something to do that can be accomplished in less than two minutes, do it right away.

8. **De-clutter your workspace.** Excess clutter leads to confusion, which leads to gridlock.

9. **Find 30 minutes of quiet time every week** to reflect on your goals and whether your choices about how to allocate your time are moving you forward at the pace you hope for.

10. **Don't stress**—there is no one way to juggle all the balls. Do the best you can. Don't waste energy and focus on worrying. Do the best you can every day and get a good night's sleep. Then repeat.

4 INTELLIGENCE

Isaac Asimov, the science fiction writer known for his high I.Q., explained that though he is thought of as highly intelligent,

> "those scores simply mean that I am very good at answering the type of academic questions that are considered worthy of answers by people who make up the intelligence tests—people with intellectual bents similar to mine."

He realized that if a mechanic, a carpenter, or a farmer made up the tests, he would score very badly because he could not use his academic training or verbal talents.

There are many different kinds of smart. Successful students recognize and use their particular types of intelligence. They also work to strengthen the kinds of intelligence they need to achieve their goals.

LEARNING STYLES

Everyone learns in his or her own way. You might remember times you've said, "I can't learn from teachers like that" or "I hate lectures." You were talking about your learning style. There are different categories of learning styles—the basic groupings are visual, auditory/aural, read-write, tactile, and kinestetic.

The **visual** learner learns best through aids such as charts, films, pictures, and highlighting with colored markers. A visual learner should try to see things in his or her head.

An **auditory** learner gets information—you guessed it—most effectively through hearing. This type of learner should use tapes, sit where lectures can be heard clearly, and verbally review information.

The **tactile** learner is the touchy-feely person. He or she might use touch to learn by tracing words and writing information that needs to be remembered.

The **kinesthetic** learner needs to involve the body to learn most effectively. He or she might take a walk while studying notes on flashcards.

The **read-write** learner likes written information. This type of learner has it the easiest in academic settings because they emphasize reading, writing, and research.

You can discover your learning style and more detailed explanations of learning styles by finding the "**Barsch Learning Inventory**" or the VARK Learning Style Inventory on the Internet.

MULTIPLE INTELLIGENCES

Howard Gardner, who developed the theory of Multiple Intelligences, defines intelligence as:

> "...the ability to solve problems, or to create products, that are valued within one or more cultural settings..."

There are several reasons why it is useful to a new college student to consider types of intelligence. One is to recognize and value your own intelligence and that of others you work and learn with; another is to develop skills to work effectively with others who may have different intelligence styles.

The following describes the strengths of Gardner's eight intelligence styles:

 Verbal-Linguistic people use language well. They like to write, tell jokes and stories, and communicate well with words.

 Logical-Mathematical people use numbers well and see patterns easily. They like technology, puzzles, and brainteasers.

 Visual-Spatial people use sight to perceive the visual world accurately. They are often best in the arts or engineering.

 Bodily-Kinesthetic people use the body and physical movement well. They like sports and projects that involve physical activity.

 Musical-Rhythmic people use a strong sense of recognition of the elements of music. They enjoy musical expression whether through singing, playing an instrument, or listening to music.

 Interpersonal people use the ability to understand, appreciate, and be sensitive to other people. They have a lot of friends and are happy in a crowd of people.

 Intrapersonal people use the ability to know themselves, examining their own strengths, weaknesses, feelings, and opinions. They like to be alone and are independent.

Naturalistic people use the ability to see patterns and categories and appreciate the items in the natural world. They like natural settings, but also are adept at organizing and collecting many kinds of items.

Emotional Intelligence involves being aware of and managing your own emotions and those of other people.

Psychologist Daniel Goleman explains that E.Q. is as important as I.Q.—and maybe even more important—in determining success in life. Even better, **although I.Q. is something we are born with and can't really change, we can improve our Emotional Intelligence throughout our lives.**

Think about the successful people you know or have heard about. They weren't necessarily the valedictorians of their high school classes, but often the ones who were confident, optimistic, popular, sensitive to the moods and feelings of others, and able to use that knowledge to control a situation. They had Emotional Intelligence.

Goleman divides **Emotional Intelligence** into two categories:

Personal Competence – Your ability to manage yourself, your emotions, and impulses. With personal competence you are self-aware so that you can understand and build on your strengths, improve your areas of weakness, delay gratification, and persist toward your goals. You can control anger and handle stress, and have the optimism to enhance your motivation.

Social Competence – Your ability to handle relationships with others. With social competence you have empathy, the ability to understand and be sensitive to the emotions of others. You can work in a team, relate to people who are different from you, persuade people, and reduce conflict.

GROAN

"A journey begins with the first step."

Groan—you've heard it a million times, but like so many of those old sayings, it is worth thinking about. Although long-term goals are important, it is hard to stick with a difficult project when you keep focusing on the scope of the task in front of you. Persistence comes with taking the first step, and then the next one, and then the next instead of being daunted by the twenty-six miles it will take to complete the marathon.

If you have a twenty-page paper to write, take comfort in knowing that you cannot write all twenty pages at once. You have to write one page at a time. Even before you start writing, you have to do your preparation, your research. By dividing your task into small pieces, scheduling the time to complete each piece, and not worrying about how much is left to do, you will be able to stick with your task. A twenty-page paper, after you have finished your preparation, is just twenty, one-page papers.

You know that you can write one page. **Start with that.**

NOTES

5 CRITICAL THINKING

"Education's purpose is to replace an empty mind with an open one."

MALCOLM S. FORBES

Did you ever drive somewhere and then wonder how you arrived, because you had no recollection of the journey? Did you ever agree to do something and then realize, too late, that it wasn't something you really wanted to do? Did you ever wonder what you were thinking—or if you were thinking?

Many of us go through our daily lives on autopilot. We don't use careful thinking and sometimes we suffer for that. Real education requires real thinking. You will be bombarded with all sorts of information, both academic and life-experience. **What will you do with that information? How will that information shape the person you are becoming?**

You need to acquire **critical-thinking skills** to get the most out of your college years.

Critical thinking is purposeful, deliberative reflection that leads us to know what to believe or do, what to accept or reject, and what to expect in the future based on present information. Critical thinking is what leads to problem-solving and making sound determinations about our own behavior.

CRITICAL THINKING: WHY?

One of the reasons you go to college is to **grow** and **change**. You especially want your thinking skills to be more sophisticated than they were when you began your higher education.

With critical-thinking skills you know how to be more deliberate in your thinking so you can **understand** and **evaluate** the information and ideas that come your way. With sharp critical-thinking skills, your opinions and the conclusions you draw will be of a higher quality.

But critical-thinking skills can be used in every subject, and in all areas of your life. Not only should they help you decide what information to believe, they should also help you to decide who to be friends with, and even whether or not to go to a certain party.

Critical-thinking skills will also be assets for a career because being able to think well and solve problems are important for any job.

Truly educated people use critical-thinking skills all the time. It is how they use the information they acquire and the experiences they have had to shape the choices they make.

GOOD NEWS: You can improve your critical-thinking skills. In fact, sharpening your thinking ability is what college is all about.

Use the acronym **ACES** to improve your critical-thinking skills:

Analyze: Read and listen carefully. Look for main ideas, supporting evidence, the differences between facts and opinions. Examine assumptions—those of others and your own. Faulty assumptions are where prejudices and bias come from.

Clarify: Make sure you understand all that data coming at you by restating what you read or what people say to you. Ask specific questions. Think about what you need to know in order to understand a situation or a problem.

Evaluate: Make decisions about the validity of the information you acquire, and whether and how you should use it. Consider the consequences of different actions. Determine the value of what you are learning, hearing, and seeing. Judge the quality of your thinking in every situation, being aware of your own fallibility and biases.

See Relationships: As E.M. Forster said: "Only connect." New information relates to other information. Look for connections between the courses you are taking, and between what you are learning now and what you have learned. Look for similarities in words and ideas, in characters and themes, in your own experiences, thoughts, and feelings. Use that information to predict or anticipate probable outcomes.

FACT OR OPINION

It is a fact that college students benefit from First-Year Experience courses.

Did I fool you? Just because someone tells you something is a fact doesn't make it so. What is a fact?

A **fact** is something that can be proved to be true **or** false.

Can we absolutely prove that every college student benefits from a First-Year Experience course? **No.**

Does that mean the statement is a lie? **No.** It is a stated opinion, presented as a fact. (So maybe it's a little lie!)

An **opinion** cannot be proved to be true or false, but can be supported by **evidence** to show its **validity**.

If the statement were to quote several studies with statistics about the benefits of a First-Year Experience course, you might agree with the opinion. **The more facts you have to back up an opinion, the more likely it is that you will convince others that you are right.** Then again, there may be many studies that show something different from the ones cited. Critical thinkers don't need to see the facts that refute a certain opinion to know that they might exist— they know there are two sides to every story.

6 NOTE-TAKING

Start off your first class of your first semester the way successful students do. **TAKE NOTES**.

Often material in a lecture will not be duplicated anywhere else. If you didn't take notes, you're sunk. Even if the lecture material duplicates the textbook, you will have recorded the parts of the readings the professor thinks are important. What do you think will be on a test?

Because you are starting a new endeavor—college—this is a good time to develop new habits.

1. **As soon as you sit down, take out paper and pen (pencil tends to fade).** Most good students keep some kind of notebook, spiral or loose-leaf, for each class. In addition to the notebook for taking notes, you want to have a place to keep handouts you've been given. Keep all materials for each class together in one place.

2. **Put the date, the topic of the lecture, and the page number at the top of the page.** Knowing where the material came in the course of the semester, and what each class or lectures was about, will help you study for exams.

IN-CLASS NOTE-TAKING SKILLS

Listen

Don't think about whether you like the lecturer's looks or styles, or whether you are bored or uninterested in the material. Just focus on the words you are hearing. Sit where you can hear well and won't be distracted. Verbal clues that tell you what to write down include the following:

- **A raised voice** – An indication of emphasis
- **Repetition** – If the instructor says something more than once, write it down!
- **Examples** – Illustrations of points or concepts
- **Definitions** – Lecturer gives meaning of words used
- **Enumerations** – "There are three characteristics you should note …"
- **Direct announcement** – "Pay attention" or "This is an essential point"

Observe

Pay attention to the lecturer's body language. He/she will give nonverbal clues as to what you should write down:

- **Writing information on the board** – Copy it
- **Using a power point** – If it is too long to copy, look for the important points
- **Gestures** – Pointing to the board, pounding on the desk, using the hands for emphasis
- **Mannerisms** – The lecturer may emphasize a particular point by an eyebrow raise, throat-clearing, or glancing at the notes

Predict and Ask Questions

Actively engage in the lecture by trying to guess what is coming next; by asking yourself questions to test your comprehension; and by trying to connect the material with things you already know.

You know what to write down—but how should you **organize** it?

You don't want your notes to be random jottings, but arranged in a way that helps you study. There are many organizational methods and you might decide which to use according to your learning style and your professor's lecture style.

Informal Outline – This organizes the material using headings that show the major topics with indentations underneath each heading that include secondary points. You might want to leave a wide margin on the side to write down further explanations or key words.

The Cornell Method – Developed by Dr. Walter Pauk, this method involves making a wide column on the left side of your paper. In the larger, right-hand section, record the important ideas from the lecture. Use the left-hand section to write down questions you have, or ideas you don't understand that you will use to fill in information and to test yourself when studying.

Clustering – This is the most visual style of note-taking. Write the speaker's first main idea in a circle in the middle of the page. Create small circles clustered around the big circle and attached by arrows for examples or secondary information that connect to the main idea. Create a new cluster for each new main idea.

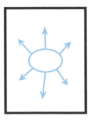

WHAT SHOULD I DO WITH MY IN-CLASS NOTES?

Although writing the information down in your notes is one step toward remembering the material, **it is not enough.**

Successful students:

- **Review notes immediately after a class.** This enables you to fill in extra information, or adjust the organization while the material is still fresh in your mind.

- **Review notes before the next class.** You will be prepared for the next lecture and have a fuller understanding of the material.

- **Review notes when studying for an exam.** You might want to use a study group and compare your notes to others to make sure you have recorded the important information.

There are many established methods of note-taking when you do your reading assignments. They include: *SQ3R, The Cornell Method, Clustering, Note Cards, Triple Underlining, and Summarizing*. It will be easy to find detailed instructions for any of these methods, but they all basically consist of three parts:

previewing, **reading**, and **organizing** the material for study.

PREVIEW + READ + ORGANIZE

Your goal is to create a study guide you can use when you have finished your reading assignment, so you never have to read that chapter again.

Whatever method you choose for organizing your reading, you should work in sections. Do not treat the entire chapter or fifty-page assignment as a whole, but divide it into chunks. Often, a chapter will already be divided by headings. Not only will it be easier to handle your material if it is in shorter sections, it will be easier for you to attack your reading assignment when your task consists of logical pieces that can be assigned allotted study times.

The three stages of the reading process take time. That is why you are expected to spend two to three hours of study time for every hour of class time.

Think of this: The more time you spend creating your **super-duper study guide**, the better it will be. The better your study guide, the better you will do on your exams!

NOTE-TAKING SKILLS FOR READING ASSIGNMENTS

Previewing

Previewing is a thorough perusal of selected parts of the reading selection that involves **asking questions** and **making predictions** before actually reading the material.

Who knew that what you do before you start your reading assignment could be so important? Good previewing helps you focus on the main points of what you are reading, enhances your understanding, and improves your recall.

When you preview, ask questions such as: Is this the topic or the main idea of the selection? What are the key words? Do I know the definitions of the key words? Make predictions such as: this is the author's point of view, this is important information, and these are the main points that will be made. When previewing, analyze the following items:

1. Title

2. Bold Headings

3. Sub-Headings

4. Introductions

5. Summaries or end-of-chapter material

6. Information about the author such as credentials and when the material was written

READING

Some people will tell you to quickly read through a section before making any marks or notations. Others will say you should highlight and/or make notations as you read that first time.

Choose what is **right for you** according to your style, the subject you are studying, and the material you are reading.

Your goals when you do the actual reading are:

Comprehension – Make sure you understand what you are reading. Look up key words that are not defined in the reading, ask yourself questions to see if you can restate the information, and connect what you read with the class lecture or to what you already know.

Selection – Through highlighting and/or explanatory notes in the margin, you are marking the material that will go into your study guide. **Don't mark everything!** Only include the material that is important enough for you to study for an exam. Summarize or restate the points in the margin when you want to consolidate the information or make comments. Do include any points that might have been made by your instructor because you know that he/she considers that material important.

ORGANIZING THE INFORMATION

The last stage of your note-taking process is organizing the information that you have highlighted or noted as you transferred the assigned material into a **study guide**.

The study guide contains only the information you think will be on an exam and that you have made sure you understand.

Once you have created your study guide, you no longer need to use the book for studying.

As always, you can use any format to organize your information. You might even find that a combination of formats works for you. You might create a study guide in outline form, but use 3x5 index cards for important terms you have to memorize. The benefit of index cards is that you can keep them with you and test yourself at random times.

An outline is often the most convenient way to arrange the information in a textbook. When you think about it, textbooks are already arranged in an outline form. They have chapter headings, section headings, and subheadings that can be transferred to your study guide as the headings for your outline.

Remember, do not put any information into your study guide that you don't understand. If a heading is confusing to you, or contains terms you don't know, **put it into your own words** and define the term when you create your **outline** so you are sure to understand everything in your study guide.

7 TEST-TAKING

Have you ever taken a test **for fun**?

Perhaps you've taken a magazine or online quiz that shows how compatible you and your romantic interest are, or how your fitness level measures up. You take those tests to find out something about yourself. Ultimately, that is what your tests in college are for—they tell you if you:

- have mastered needed information
- can apply what you know to solve problems
- remember critical facts
- can communicate information effectively
- understand the topics in a course
- are ready to move on
- can connect new information to old

Tests can also be a **wake-up call**: an hour's studying just isn't going to do it;

neither is an occasional appearance in class or sporadic completion of assignments. Tests help clarify and reinforce your knowledge of the subject, so they are learning experiences in themselves.

Tests also tell your instructor a great deal about how well she/he has been teaching the course and if she/he needs to spend more time on certain areas. In addition, of course, they tell the instructor the same things about you that you learned about yourself. Finally, they enable the teacher to have an objective basis on which to give you a grade.

Although we'd like to think that the learning is all that counts, **GRADES MATTER**. They are an assessment of your performance in college that transfer or graduate schools and future employers will look at when they decide whether to accept or hire you. **They become part of your permanent record—that paperwork that will follow you around all your life.** Twenty years from now, when you apply for a job or another degree, a company or a college may still want to see that transcript from college.

You can **improve your test-taking skills**.

There are **three steps** to the process.

TEST-TAKING STEP ONE: PREPARATION

1. **Begin preparing** for your tests from the first day of class by attending all classes and taking good notes. If you must miss a class, get the notes from a reliable classmate as soon as possible.

2. **Do all assignments.** Create study guides for the assigned readings. Make a list of things that you don't understand to ask the professor during class.

3. **Find out** what topics and material will be covered on the test.

4. **Combine** class notes, handouts, and study guides from reading assignments into one guide. Create a one-page review sheet to look over before going to sleep the night before, and in the last minutes before your test.

5. **Find out what kind of questions** will be on the test: essay, multiple-choice, short answer?

6. **Make a study schedule** that allocates study times for several days before the test.

7. **Use memory techniques** and allow enough time to memorize terms, formulas, dates, etc.

8. **Go to instructors' office hours,** the tutoring center, or meet with a study group to review and clarify material you don't understand.

9. **Create a pretest** using questions at the end of chapters, questions the professor has asked, and questions you make up. Take your test and allow enough time to correct it and review areas of weakness.

10. **Sleep and eat.** Your brain needs to be rested and fueled in order to function at its best.

TEST-TAKING STEP TWO: TAKING THE TEST

1. **Arrive a little early** so you can choose a good seat (good light, temperature, noise level, away from distractions), relax, and look over your review sheet.

2. **Preview** the exam.

3. **Write down information**, such as formulas or definitions, which you have memorized and might forget during the exam.

4. **Plan your time**, leaving time for review. Spend the most time on questions that are worth the most!

5. **Careful reading** is an essential test-taking skill.

   > Read directions carefully. Note when a question has more than one part. Note where you are to put the T or F in a true/false test. Note if you are directed to answer a certain number of questions rather than all of them.

   > Read questions carefully. Circle key words that tell you what to do, such as "list" or "define." Make sure you answer the question that is asked. Watch for key words such as "why" that asks for a reason, or "what" that asks for an explanation. Pay attention to the words used in the questions. If you don't know the definitions, make your best guess at the meanings using context clues. Think about other questions that have been asked— you may find hints to the current question in other questions.

6. **Answer the easy questions first** but stick to your schedule allowing enough time for all the questions.

7. **Write clearly**. If the instructor can't read what you've written, she or he will probably mark it wrong.

8. **Review the test** when you are finished. Reread the questions. Make sure you've looked at both sides of the paper and haven't skipped anything. Read your answers carefully. **Don't leave early**. (And don't be distracted by students who do leave early—that doesn't mean they'll do well on the test!)

9. **Be willing to change an answer,** but only if you are positive it is wrong. Often the first guess is the right one.

10. **Don't cheat**. You will defeat all the purposes of testing, including the gathering of information about your progress that is valuable for you. Plus, you will eventually get caught! Do you want to think of yourself as a cheater?

1. **Do not look at your grade** and stuff the test into your backpack. A completed test is an extremely valuable learning experience. Pat yourself on the back if you did well. Curse under your breath if you did poorly.

2. **Read the instructor's comments.** They will indicate areas that were troublesome for you. Look at the questions you got wrong. Look for trends.

3. **Analyze your mistakes.** Are there certain types of questions that gave you trouble? Did you not understand some of the material? Were you missing materials because of poor class notes or incomplete study guides? Were wrong answers due to poor reading of directions or questions? Did you make careless errors? Did you prepare well enough? If you did well on the test, analyze that also. What did you do right? You want to be able to duplicate the results on other tests.

4. **Be honest** and sincere about what areas need improvement.

5. **Even though the test is over**, get help on the areas that you do not understand. Much of learning is cumulative. If you haven't mastered one stage before moving on to the next, you will be in real trouble as the semester goes on.

6. **Remember**, a test is an objective assessment of how well you have mastered certain material. It says nothing about your value as a person. Do not let a bad grade get you down. But also remember that you should not be a passive victim. You can get better grades if you actively set about making changes in your test-taking behavior.

7. **Ask** about any opportunity to take a make-up test to raise your grade.

8. **Talk** with your instructor (politely) if you feel that there are mistakes in the grading.

9. **Reward yourself** for good results. You want to reinforce your own good test-taking behaviors.

10. **Save your test.** You may need it as a study guide for the next test, or a midterm or final.

Tests can be divided into two types: **recognition** and **recall**.

Recognition tests are the objective kinds of tests: multiple choice, true/false, and matching.

You must recognize the correct answer from the choices given. Find out if points will be deducted for wrong answers; if not, guess and do not leave any questions blank. If it is a true/false test, for instance, you have a **50/50** chance of being right.

Recall tests are the more subjective tests: essays, short answers, and fill-in-the-blanks.

You must supply the information, or recall it from your memory. In the case of essays, and to a lesser extent short answers, you must also use that information, connecting it to other information to create a response. Find out if partial credit will be given for your answers. If so, write as fully and completely as possible about the topic in the hope that you will get something right.

Sherlock Holmes said:

"WHENEVER YOU ELIMINATE THE IMPOSSIBLE, whatever remains, however improbable, **must be the truth**."

He could have been talking about one of the **strategies** for taking multiple-choice tests. There are techniques to help you optimize your results:

- Read the question carefully, **underlining** key words.

- Try to answer **without looking** at the choices. If your answer is among the choices, it is probably correct.

- **Eliminate** the obvious wrong choices to enhance your odds of getting the right answer.

- Read each of the answers carefully, watching for **extreme qualifying words** such as "always" and "never." Those choices are usually wrong. Watch for negatives such as "which of the following is *not*…" Watch for statements such as "all but one," which mean the majority of the options are *correct* except for the right answer.

- Options with **moderate modifying words** such as "often," "most," or "may sometimes be" are often the right answer.

- If two options seem correct, and you have to guess, choose the one that is **longest and most complete**.

- If two options are the same, neither is correct unless there is a choice that **includes both**. For example:
  a. Six
  b. Half-dozen
  c. Both a and b
  d. None of the above

- If two options are **similar**, one is probably correct.

- If two options are **opposite**, one is often right.

- The correct answer should work **grammatically** to complete the sentence started by the question.

- **If you are positive** that two answers are correct, the "all of the above" choice is probably the right one.

TRUE/FALSE QUESTIONS

- **Read every word.** Wrong answers are often the result of missing negatives, or thinking a statement is true when only part of it is true. For a statement to be true, every part of it must be true, while a statement can be false if only a small part is false.

- Watch for those **extreme qualifiers** such as *always, only,* or *every*. Statements containing them are usually false.

- Statements containing **moderate qualifiers** such as *often, usually,* or *some* are often true.

- Watch for **oversimplification** and **generalizations**. These statements that try to indicate cause and effect or mask complexity are often false.

MATCHING QUESTIONS

- **Read directions carefully**, noting whether you can use items more than once and whether there is the same number of items in both lists.

- **Work from one column.** If you work from the column with the longer entries, it will save time when you read for matches.

- Start with the **matches you know**.

- Apply all **grammar rules** to find the best match.

FILL-IN-THE-BLANK OR SENTENCE COMPLETION QUESTIONS

- Read the question carefully, looking for **key words**.

- Read your answer carefully, making sure it **fits into the sentence** properly.

- Pay attention to the length and number of the blanks. The answer may not be an **exact fit**, but chances are it will be close.

- **Look for clues.** Is there an "an" before the blank? Then the answer begins with a vowel. Does the verb indicate that the answer is singular or plural?

`<blank>`

These questions often strike fear into the hearts of students, but if you follow the steps of **planning**, **writing**, and **revising**, you can handle the challenge.

Treat your test essays as you would any essay: provide a thesis and support and write clearly.

Your goal is to figure out exactly what the question is. It takes some analysis and careful reading. **Ask yourself these three questions:**

1. What task does this question ask me to perform? The clue lies in directive words such as: analyze, compare, define, discuss, summarize, and explain.

2. What is the topic of this question? Look for a word or phrase that tells you exactly what the subject is.

3. What hints does the question give me about my response? Does it ask for certain details to be included? Does it ask for a certain number of reasons to support a claim?

Answering these questions is part of your planning stage. Your thesis will be your answer to the question.

Plan your essay using the brainstorming and outlining techniques for any writing project. Your thesis must be clear and your support specific, using the information you have learned about the topic. Budget your time, making sure you will have a chance to review and revise.

Write using a structure that includes an introduction, supporting evidence, and a conclusion.

Revise checking for clarity, that you have answered all parts of the question, and that your thesis is a genuine response to the essay question.

OVERCOMING TEST ANXIETY

Everyone gets nervous about tests. Some level of anxiety is helpful, making you perform at your best. But too much anxiety can make you feel sick and unable to concentrate.

There are techniques that work to help relieve some of your test anxiety. The more you apply these techniques, the more positively reaffirming testing experiences you'll have!

1. **Cultivate a positive attitude.** Remember, tests are not a measure of your value as a person. You are not doomed to repeat past performances—you do have the power to change.

2. **Prepare thoroughly.** If you feel confident that you have done what you can to succeed, you will be more confident about taking the test. Some of the worst anxiety occurs in students who are unprepared.

3. **Use your instructors** as allies—go for help.

4. **Find study partners** who are not necessarily your friends, but people who will help you do your best.

5. **Sit far away** from other students who might make you nervous. Pay no attention to pretest chatter.

6. **Use relaxation techniques** such as deep breathing, visualizing a good grade, and tightening and releasing muscles.

7. **Divide the questions** and your time into chunks. Applaud yourself when you complete each section.

You will need to memorize material for your tests in college.

Memory is a complicated process that involves short-term, or working memory, and long-term memory. You need to focus on one thing at a time in order to record information into short-term memory.

To transfer information into long-term memory so that you can retrieve it for a test and for further use:

Repeat – Not the most powerful technique, but works better if you try to use the information instead of going over it again and again.

Overlearn – Keep working with the information even after you think you've learned it.

Chunk – Study smaller pieces of information over a longer stretch of time.

Remember the Middle – We tend to pay more attention to beginning and ends.

Feel – Engage your emotions and personalize.

Connect – Connect new information to things you already know.

Create Mnemonics – Use memory tricks such as acronyms.

Use Kinesthetic learning – Mark up tests, write things down, create maps and charts, act things out, make the information funny.

NOTES

8 MIDTERM

You are now **halfway** through your first semester.

This is a great time to turn your critical-thinking skills on yourself. Use your **ACES strategy** (analyze, clarify, evaluate, see relationships) in a purposeful and deliberate way, reflecting on the following areas:

1. Your ACADEMIC PROGRESS
2. Your GOALS and your PROGRESS toward meeting them
3. Your PERSONAL PROGRESS
4. Your FUTURE

YOUR ACADEMIC PROGRESS

You have received your midterm grades by now, or have some other indication of how you are doing. Grades don't evaluate whether you are kind, interesting, funny, or decent—the criteria most of us use in judging others. What they do show is how well you are playing the game of college. To win this game, you have to be purposeful about following the principles of being a successful student:

- BE THERE
- DO THE WORK
- GET HELP
- PLAN
- THINK

If your performance needs improvement, can you trace any problems to a lack of attention to the factors above? Remember, success is largely a matter of persevering in the right way. Perhaps you have had trouble understanding the content of a course, or trouble with a particular instructor's teaching style. Did you go for help or just allow matters to get worse?

Hoping things will get better doesn't make them change. You have to **take action** if you want **better results**.

If your midterm grades are good, congratulations! However, a good performance brings its own perils. In some subjects, the work gets more difficult as the semester goes on. Figure out what you have done that has been so effective, and rededicate yourself to following the principles of success.

Halfway through your first college semester is an excellent time to re-evaluate your goals.

Do you still want what you thought you did? Were you realistic about what you hoped to attain? Do you need to readjust, or even completely **change your direction**?

Perhaps one of your goals was to be on the Dean's List your first year, yet you have discovered that, despite following the principles of being a successful student, you have gotten a C- midterm grade. Perhaps it is more realistic for your goal to be spending a certain number of hours in the tutoring center, or even for you to bring that grade up from a C- to a B- by the end of the semester.

Conversely, perhaps you haven't worked very hard but have attained a B average. Maybe you see the possibility of being on the Dean's List if you work a little harder, and would like to add that to your short-term goals.

Goals should always be re-evaluated. Establish the habit of making midterm one of those times you consider where you are going and how well you are proceeding down the path.

How **YOU** doin'?

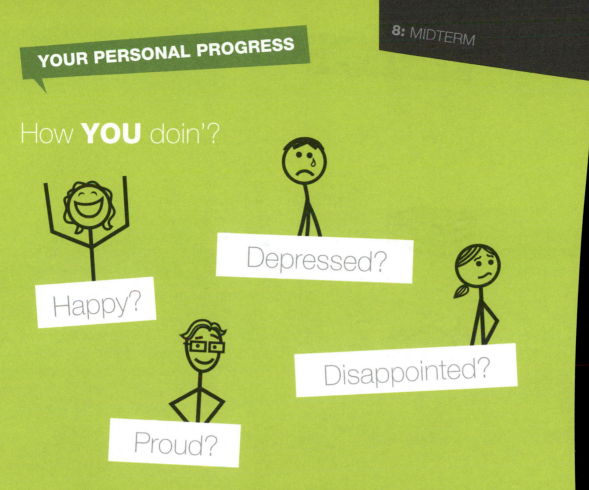

Happy?

Depressed?

Disappointed?

Proud?

Are you a little more grown-up than you were a few months ago? How are you handling time management? Have you been behaving wisely in regard to your health, safety, and finances? Are you behaving in accord with your own personal values? Do those values need some readjusting?

How about the new people you've met? Are the relationships you've formed helping or hurting you? Are you allowing yourself to branch out and learn from the many kinds of people you are being exposed to now?

College is not just about academic growth but personal growth as well.

Have you created some beneficial new habits? Stayed away from behaviors that might become bad habits? Thrown out old baggage you don't need anymore? Not too much time has passed, so it should be easy to make changes you see are needed.

Now is the time to start thinking about:

> **Courses For Next Semester.** Re-examining your goals should help you with these decisions. Seek advice from counselors, professors, fellow students, and Web sites. Register as early as you are allowed in order to have your choice of courses and schedules.

> **Next Year's Living Situation.** Residential students need to request dorms or find apartments surprisingly early. Be proactive in creating the best living situation for yourself. Commuting students should also consider their living arrangements. Is it time to leave home? Or should you move back home?

> **Finances.** If you are getting financial aid, make sure your paperwork is in order. Apply for grants. Think about reducing work hours or getting an on-campus job if working has harmed your school performance. Consider a job or volunteer work if you are not spending your free time wisely.

> **Student Activities.** Perhaps you were too overwhelmed at the beginning of the semester to consider the array of clubs, activities, and services available to students. But there are many things going on at college that will help you make friends, enjoy hobbies, further career goals, improve your school performance, improve your health and fitness, or help you give back to the community. Join something!

> **Summer.** Now is the time to check out jobs, internships, and summer school possibilities. If you wait too long, opportunities will be gone.

WHAT'S NEXT?
9 MAJORS AND CAREERS

John Lennon said,

"LIFE IS WHAT HAPPENS TO YOU when you are busy **making other plans.**"

And, in some respects, that is true about choosing a career.

Of course you need to start thinking about how you would like to spend your adult years—those 40 years on average between your entry into the workforce until retirement. But, you should **not** feel that the decisions you make today (as a first-year student) are going to bind you to a commitment you may wish to change. Most people hold seven or eight jobs during their working years.

A recent study indicated that only **two percent** of the people surveyed claim to be working in the occupation they had planned when they were eighteen years old. That seems very low—but the point is that you need to remain flexible and open-minded.

Here is our best advice for now:

Start researching careers and opportunities centered on activities you enjoy doing and that you are good at. You probably have some **big-picture ideas** as to the right kind of career for you. Within those categories, start researching the various choices and options you may have upon graduation.

"The reason adults are always asking children what they want to be when they grow up is because they are looking for ideas."

PAULA POUNDSTONE

Most schools encourage you to choose a major at the end of your first year. As we have noted, you should not feel that this choice locks you in. However, at the same time, you do want to start building on your knowledge in a specific area.

The world is moving away from **generalists** (people with a whole variety of disciplines), and toward **specialists** (people with a lot of knowledge about one particular area).

Now is also the time to explore the career development offices at your school. Once you have a sense of the type of activities you would like to build a career, talking to those who have traveled before you can be helpful. Access the experience of advisors at your school who can help you hone in on career options and the kind of curriculum and major that will enhance your development in that area.

FINDING MENTORS

Effective people know that you rarely have to reinvent the wheel.

Whatever you are doing or wish to do, there are people who have already done it. These people are potential mentors.

A **mentor** is anyone who will give you some of his or her time to guide your passage to the career(s) you are interested in. A mentor might be a graduate student, a teacher, or even someone unrelated to your school who is working in your area(s) of choice.

How do you approach a mentor?

Be straightforward and direct (and polite!). More people will respond positively than you might think.

Find someone who is doing what you want to do.

Ask for ten minutes of their time to give you some personal advice.

Respect their time and don't go beyond what you committed to.

At the end of the ten minutes, ask if they would be willing to receive future questions from you. If so, you have the beginning of a mentoring relationship. If not, ask if they have suggestions of someone who might be open to helping you. **If you don't ask, you will never know!**

Internships can take a variety of forms, but in general they are any situation where you learn by doing (often without pay).

Whether during the school year or during summer break, if you can put yourself in a position to try out your career interest, you are going to realize several benefits:

1. You will gain insight into what the typical day in that career is like.

2. You will begin to meet people who might help you in the future.

3. You may find the activity in that career is not what you hoped for.

There is a great book titled **Flow**, written by Mihaly Csikszentmihalyi. The message of this book is that the happiest people in life are those who are doing what they love to do. The word "**flow**" refers to the state of contentment in activity—when you lose track of time, when you forget to eat, when you don't hear dogs barking.

If you can find the path to a career where you will experience "flow," you will most likely be very successful… **and content**. An internship is one great way to do that.

WRITING EFFECTIVE RÉSUMÉS

Of course at some point you will need to get a job. And in that process you will most likely have to give someone your **résumé**, essentially an outline of why you are qualified for the position you desire.

Use these tips for preparing a résumé:

1. **There is a form for résumés that most employers are used to seeing**—your school's career office will likely have forms for you to look at.

2. **Don't get too hung up on one form**, however. There is no one right form.

3. **Highlight points that will be of interest** to a prospective employer. Be careful not to overload the résumé with irrelevant information.

4. **Humanize your résumé**—ultimately the employer wants to hire someone he or she can relate to.

You need to assume that the job you are applying for is very popular and that there are many applicants.

So, you need to create a cover letter that **separates you** from the pack. Something that will grab the prospective employer's attention and cause him or her to read further and look at your résumé.

Here's some advice for writing a powerful cover letter:

1. Don't dally. Your first sentence should say exactly why you are writing.

2. Less is more! Do not overwhelm the reader with too much text. People tend to pull away from lots of reading, even before they get into the substance.

3. Write and then rewrite. Your cover letter will get better with each revision. Oh yes, after your rewrite, do so again.

4. End with a call to action: "I look forward to hearing from you… my e-mail is…" Make it as easy as possible for the reader of your cover letter to contact you.

INTERVIEWS

The interview is probably the **most important** part of the hiring process. Good cover letters and résumés get you in the door, but the interview is where you can shine.

Advice for interviews:

1. **Just be you.** You can't (and don't want to) disguise the true you.

2. **Address the interviewer's questions**—listen carefully to help you discern exactly what he or she wants to know.

3. **Don't be afraid to express how much you want the opportunity.** Don't play coy, and be careful of asking too many questions; you might give the impression that you're weighing other options. Tell the interviewer how much you want the position.

4. **When you sense the interview is over, don't linger.** Don't let the interviewer push you out; leave him or her wanting to spend more time with you.

5. **In closing, ask about the next step.** Ask whether there is more you can provide to help your chances.

10 READING AND WRITING

duh

"I learned how to read and write way back in grammar school," you may be thinking. You did. And those skills have taken you to where you are now, but at this point you're going to have to **step it up!**

The sheer amount of pages you will be assigned to read, and essays, journals, reflection pieces, analyses, discussions, and explanations you will have to write, require that you pay more attention to your skills in reading and writing. Just as you have learned about being more conscious of your thinking by using critical-thinking skills, you should also develop **critical-reading** and **critical-writing** skills.

READING

One of the most useful things you can do right now is find out how long it takes to read a page.

Choose a full page from a textbook and time yourself as you read it carefully. It might take anywhere from two to five minutes, or even longer. Now, when you get that fifty-page reading assignment, you can be more accurate in planning your time.

Before deciding how to address a reading assignment, it is important to consider the **genre** of the reading selection and the **writer's purpose**.

Why is it important to be aware of the genre of what you are reading?
Would you read a comic book the same way you read a current-event article? Would you read a poem the same way that you read a chapter in your Organic Chemistry textbook? Probably, without even realizing it, you have already been employing different skills to read different materials. But you can be a more effective reader if you are conscious of the different skills that you should use.

The broadest distinction in genre is between fiction and nonfiction. People tend to say that nonfiction is true and fiction is untrue, yet many works of literature contain greater truths than an outdated biology textbook. If you think of fiction as works of the imagination, and nonfiction as works based on fact, you are closer to a useful definition. Yet, even then, many essays, memoirs, biographies, and even articles contain so many of the elements of fiction, they are dubbed "creative nonfiction." The skills that are useful for reading fiction should often be applied to these works as well.

Welcome to the world of blurry borders that you will encounter more and more as you engage in **higher-level thinking!**

We want to identify the different genres of writing because different genres are written for different purposes. The writer of a textbook has very different intentions than the writer of a graphic novel. The purpose is the reason the writer wrote the selection. When you consider what result the writer was seeking, you can apply specific reading skills that will help you get the fullest comprehension out of what you read. In addition, applying different reading skills to different types of writing will help you do well when you have to use the material for tests or papers.

There are **three general purposes** that are useful for a reader to consider: *information*, *persuasion*, and *entertainment*.

There is usually overlap in purpose. A writer of an essay may primarily be trying to persuade, but she also may use humor or tell a suspenseful story to entertain her reader and capture his attention. There are those blurry borders again!

INFORMATION

Much of the reading you will do in college is meant to inform. This kind of reading will usually be followed by some kind of test for which you must demonstrate that you have understood the information, and that you can recall the important facts, concepts, and ideas. **When you read for information your goal is to create a study guide to use when you study for your test.**

There are many techniques, such as SQ3R, that have traditionally been taught to help people read for information. All these techniques employ the following basic steps:

Preview (see next page)

If the material is more than a couple of pages, preview and read a section at a time.

Read

This is the step when you actually read all the words in order to comprehend the material and choose the important information to put in your study guide. As you read, look for the answers to questions you posed in the previewing step. Highlight those answers and other important information that you think you need to know for the test. Make notes in the margins or on index cards of concepts, ideas, and definitions that you want to have in your study guide.

Organize the information

Take the important material you selected during your reading and create your study guide using whatever form works for you. You might make an outline, create index cards, make a graphic organizer, or use a combination of techniques. **You can use the headings and subheadings in the chapter to serve as the organizing structure for your study guide.**

Review

Otherwise known as memorizing or studying, this step is when you work with your study guide to enter the information into your long-term memory so it is available for a test or a paper.

Previewing is the careful consideration of a reading selection before you read it.

Often overlooked, this step can increase comprehension and save time when you are actually reading the text. If you have ever tried to organize a stack of papers, you can understand the beauty of previewing. Instead of trying to figure out where everything should go as you weed through your stack, imagine if you had a drawer full of folders that were neatly labeled with every possible category your papers could fit in. You only have to drop the right paper in the right folder as you quickly breeze through your pile. **Think of previewing as making those file folders.**

Begin by reading the title.

Examine every word of that title; look up any of the key words you don't know; ask yourself questions about the title such as "what does the author mean by that phrase?" Make predictions about the title such as whether it might indicate the topic or main idea of the piece, or if it shows the author's opinion of the subject. Write your questions and predictions down so you can focus on them when you read.

After you have thoroughly considered the title, carefully read whichever following items are applicable to your text, continuing to ask questions and make predictions:

1. Introduction
2. Bold headings
3. Subheadings
4. Concluding materials
5. Biographical material about the author
6. Extra information about the selection such as when and where it was written

PERSUASION

Essays are probably the first thing that come to mind when you think of persuasive writing, but there is an element of persuasion in many kinds of writing that might seem objective (newspaper articles), entertaining (novels), or widely accepted as true (works in psychology or philosophy).

Persuasive writing calls upon your best critical-thinking skills because it is trying to mess with your mind. **Before you allow someone's words to cause you to believe, think, or do something, you should evaluate the argument very carefully.**

1. **Identify** whether a selection or a part of a selection is persuasive. Is there a thesis, an opinion, or a selection of information employed to make you think or believe something? Is the author seducing you with words to make you see things the way he or she does?

2. **Find out about the author.** Look for credentials or expertise that would make you give serious consideration to what he or she says.

3. **Withhold your agreement** until you have carefully examined the support of the author's opinions and ideas. What kind of evidence does the author use to prove his or her points? Does it stand up in your court or could you challenge its validity?

4. **Open your mind** to accepting new thoughts and opinions that stand up to your challenges. Being persuaded by worthy ideas is one of the exciting parts of education.

You may doubt the entertainment value of any kind of reading, but even Shakespeare was writing to keep an audience enthralled.

Novels, plays, poetry, and short stories are the kinds of works we think of as meant to be entertaining, but essays, memoirs, and even magazine articles need to keep the reader interested.

It might help to understand writing that is meant to entertain if you expand your definition of entertainment to **enlightenment**.

This kind of writing casts a light on certain truths about life and people without directly telling you what to think. Writing for entertainment appeals to the senses and the emotions to make you feel or know these things, instead of depending on argument. Even the trashiest romance novel or the bloodiest thriller has something to say about love or good and evil.

Your job as the reader of entertaining writing is to spot the truths that are presented to you using all or some of the following elements:

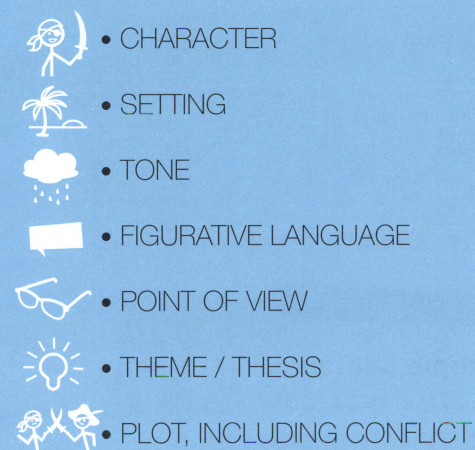

- CHARACTER

- SETTING

- TONE

- FIGURATIVE LANGUAGE

- POINT OF VIEW

- THEME / THESIS

- PLOT, INCLUDING CONFLICT

There is an element of persuasion in writing meant for entertainment. Once you discover what the work is saying, it's up to you to decide whether or not to accept the truth of such observations about life and humanity based on your own emotions, observations, and experiences.

In order to understand what you read you have to be able to **identify** the topics and main ideas of paragraphs and of whole works.

> **Topic:** This is the subject of a paragraph or selection. The question to ask to identify a topic is: Who or what is this about? The answer should come in a word or phrase such as **cell division, depression, the cost of health care, the difference between topic** and **main idea.**

> **Main Idea:** This is what the paragraph or selection says about the topic. The question to ask to identify the main idea is: What point does the author make about the topic? The answer should come in a complete sentence such as **"The difference between topic and main idea is that topic is a subject, expressed in a word or phrase, and main idea is a complete thought, expressed in a sentence."**

TOPIC SENTENCE

Topic Sentence: This term applies **only** to paragraphs.

It is the sentence that expresses the main idea of a paragraph. Topic sentences are the most important and most general sentences in the paragraph, and should relate to all the other sentences in the paragraph.

Not all paragraphs have topic sentences. These handy devices make it very easy for a reader to understand the point of a paragraph. (It's good to use topic sentences in your writing too, to increase your clarity.)

Topic sentences can be found anywhere in the paragraph, but they are often the first sentence. If you begin reading every difficult paragraph by testing if the first sentence contains the main idea, you will find that just searching for the topic sentence aids your comprehension.

WRITING

Almost all students are required to take at least one composition course that ensures they have the basic writing skills to do college-level work. These skills boil down to the ability to write essays and papers that contain a thesis supported by various types of evidence, and that are expressed clearly using proper grammar, syntax, and word choice.

What some students don't take enough notice of (critical thinking) is that all the ingredients of good writing are contained in what they read. It seems like such a simple equation, but it's so true:

The **more** you read, the **better** you will write.

Remember those basic reading terms: topic, main idea, topic sentence? They are the building blocks of your writing.

Writing is a process. Writing anything worth reading (and why would you hand in something that wasn't worth reading?) is a process composed of many steps. Most students would say the hardest part of writing an essay or a paper is beginning. But if you think of your task as working your way through a series of steps, starting your paper is as easy as doing Step 1.

The Writing Process

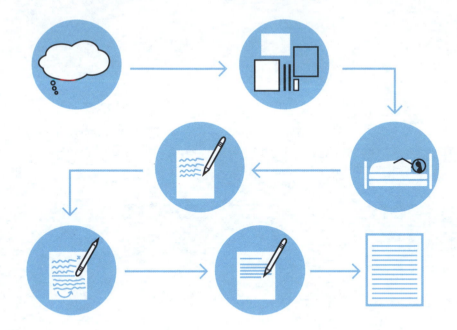

1. PLANNING

2. PREPARING

3. RESTING

4. WRITING THE FIRST DRAFT

5. REVISING

6. EDITING

As with reading, you will probably want to divide a long writing assignment into sections, but be sure to read through your paper from beginning to end when you edit so that you are assured of good continuity.

HINT: GOOD WRITING TAKES TIME.

When students do not plan the time to go through each step of the writing process, the result is an essay or a paper that is poorly researched, poorly written, or does not fulfill the assignment. It's awful to know that you could have done better if you had spent more time.

Completing Step 1 takes care of the time issue while making it easy to begin your assignment. **As soon as you get your assignment:**

- **READ YOUR ASSIGNMENT CAREFULLY.** How long is the paper supposed to be? When is it due? What questions are being asked? Do you have to do research or get materials on reserve at the library?

- **THINK ABOUT THE ASSIGNMENT.** What do you need to do to complete your paper? Can you get a feel for the thesis you will be pursuing, or a direction you want to go in your research?

- **MAKE A SCHEDULE.** Take out your planner and put down exactly when you will go to the library, create an outline, write your first draft, and complete the steps in the writing process. This schedule will make your writing task much easier and ensure that you have enough time to do a good job.

PREPARE.

This step is so easy you don't even have to procrastinate.

The goal of this step is for you to have everything you need when you sit down to write, including materials such as cartridges and paper, or the means and ability to create a PowerPoint presentation. (You may need to find someone to help you.) Your main task in this step is to do your research and take notes so you have all the information you need to complete your assignment.

Take good notes! When you have completed your preparation step, you do not want to have to go back to the sources.

A WORD ABOUT PLAGIARISM: Even with the most honest intentions, it is hard to avoid using the thoughts or words of others. Unless an idea is common knowledge (found in many sources) attribute it to the source.

- **Use your own words when you take notes** so when you write the paper you will already have avoided quoting the source without attribution. If there are phrases that you want to quote, put quotation marks in your notes.

- **Record the citation for each source immediately.** You should have a scrupulous record of every source you have consulted. Find out what type of citation your instructor wants you to use and get the format from your library or online.

RESTING.

You may worry that you are goofing off when you want to take a break or get away from your work. Sometimes you are goofing off, but sometimes you are doing the necessary resting that allows your unconscious to work with the information you have assembled during preparation and make connections. Writing for college may not seem like creative work, but it is, and creative work depends on these interludes when the brain does its work behind the scenes. Most writers find that when they step away from the work they come back with new ideas.

Just don't step away for too long—and be sure to come back!

WRITING.

The moment when you actually have to sit down at the keyboard or paper and write is the hardest. Break this step into smaller pieces.

- **Brainstorm.** Write down your topic and record all your thoughts about that topic as you scan your notes. Write down any main ideas that occur to you. Ask yourself questions to focus your ideas.
- **Organize your ideas.** Make an outline or a map of the information you have jotted down. What ideas go together? What examples or evidence go together? Start molding your outline until you have organized it into a thesis with supporting points.
- **Free write.** Write whatever comes to mind, based on the thoughts and ideas you have organized. Do not listen to your self-censor at this stage—just let it flow.
- **Apply critical reading skills to your free write.** Read over what you have written and look for a sound thesis and evidence that you can develop as support.
- **Create a working thesis statement.** This is the main idea, or the point you will make about the topic. The thesis will guide you in writing your essay or paper.
- **Write your first draft. Don't think of this as a rough draft.** Most likely, your final product will be a revision of this draft. It should be as good as you can make it from the beginning. Your free write was for spontaneous expression; be more deliberate about the first draft. *Hint: Try to use topic sentences so you know that each paragraph makes a point that is relevant.*

You do not have to write an entire essay or paper in one sitting. You can divide this step into chunks, handling one section at a time. For instance, you might give yourself an hour to write the introduction in the morning, and two hours to write the body in the afternoon. Remember— schedule enough time to write well.

REVISING.

There is a difference between editing and revising. Revising is not tweaking, it's **surgery**.

This is the stage when you make major additions and deletions. You may move sections around or completely rephrase sentences that are not clear. **Your goal in revision is to make sure that there is a clear point in each paragraph,** and that each paragraph contributes to the main points of your writing. You should have no confusion about the thesis or main points, and neither should your reader.

1. **Reread the assignment.** Make sure you know exactly what questions your writing is supposed to answer and what information should be included.

2. **Print your work.** Reading hard copy is very different from reading off the screen.

3. **Read it out loud.** Yes, you will feel like an idiot until you spot those sentences that make no sense when you hear them.

4. **Look for thesis or main ideas, and evidence.** Do you make and support your points? Are your points clear? Is your evidence specific? Do you have ideas that do not contribute, that distract, or that actually damage what you are trying to say? Be ruthless—delete. Do you need more or better support?

NOTE: If your instructor has read a draft and made comments, be sure to incorporate those comments at this stage.

5. **Look for clarity.** Should you rearrange the order of what you have presented? Does each sentence make a clear point that a reader (who is not inside your head) will understand? Is your grammar correct or are there run-on sentences and disagreement between subject and verb that will muddy a reader's comprehension of your writing?

EDITING.

You are almost there. Your major pieces are in place on your paper or essay.

This stage is where you make it pretty.

- Read through your work from **beginning to end**.

- Look for further **grammatical errors** such as verb tense problems.

- Look for **misspelled words**. You cannot only rely on spell-check—it will not fix the mistake if you have confused "there" and "their."

- Check **punctuation**. Are quotation marks used correctly?

- Check for **typos** and **other errors** such as skipped numbers in a list.

- Check **form** and **accuracy** in footnotes and citations.

- Check that the **format** is as required in such areas as the cover page or page numbering.

Put the paper in your book bag and **celebrate** the completion of a good piece of work.

11 SPEAKING

There is nothing more **compelling** than a well-stated oral presentation.

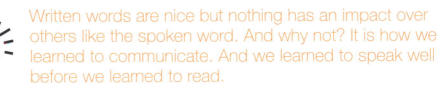

Written words are nice but nothing has an impact over others like the spoken word. And why not? It is how we learned to communicate. And we learned to speak well before we learned to read.

One element of your growth as a college student should be the development of oral presentation skills. And here is something very important to know: **Most great speakers are not naturals.** They were not born with an ability to hold an audience's attention.

Rather, they worked at their skills. They realized the importance of public speaking and made a conscious effort to develop their talents.

"All the great speakers were bad speakers first."

RALPH WALDO EMERSON

TIPS FOR EFFECTIVE SPEAKING

Below are five tips to make your oral presentations as effective as possible:

1. **Less is more.** You know how short your attention span is, so assume that your listeners' attention span is even shorter. Leave your audience wanting more. When you err on length, err on the side of too short.

2. **Interlace your comments with personal experiences.** People love stories. Don't be afraid of appearing stupid in your narratives. We all appreciate people who can laugh at themselves. We all do dumb stuff.

3. **Try to speak without notes for the first and last minutes of your presentation.** You don't need to memorize your comments verbatim. But, it would be nice if you could speak from the cuff at least in your opening and closing.

4. **Speak slowly and look at people.** Scan the audience. Connect with your listener as much as you can.

5. **Try to end with a high point.** What thought do you want to leave your listener with?

Public speaking is an acquired skill. Learning just a few tricks and tips can make you much more **effective**.

Many people are frightened of public speaking. In fact, it ranks right up there with the fear of snakes and heights.

No one in the audience is going to bite you. And it is highly unlikely that you will fall off the stage and hurt yourself. **So, what is the fear about?**

It is about embarrassment. It is about looking silly. Okay, that's understandable, but the fact is that we all do dumb stuff. We all look silly at times. So what? People understand and relate to those who screw up. In fact, making mistakes can be really endearing.

So, just prepare as well as you can (more on that to follow), walk out there and do your best. **You just might surprise yourself!**

PRACTICE, PRACTICE, PRACTICE

There is no better way to enhance your performance and get over any jitters than to **practice, practice, practice** before you ever start speaking a word in public.

Every great speaker **practices** before he or she takes the stage. The idea that people are natural **"ad-libbers"** is a myth.

There are several reasons why practice makes perfect when it comes to public speaking:

1. The more you practice, the more you hone your comments. The content of your speech will improve with each run-through.

2. The more you practice, the more comfortable you will be on "game day." After you have rehearsed your comments (in front of a mirror is good), you become more at ease with the delivery.

3. The more you practice, the more able you are to think on your feet. This one may seem counterintuitive, but the fact is, the more you prepare (practice), the more able you are to vary from the script—you are comfortable when you take the stage and your creative juices can flow.

As with any skill, the more you do it, the better you get at it. The same is true for public speaking. If one of the greatest orators of all time, Demosthenes, can rehearse with pebbles in his mouth (or so the stories go) so he was able to enunciate more clearly when he gave a speech, then certainly the rest of us can practice a bit, too.

THREE THICK THISTLE STICKS
three thick thistle sticks
three thick thistle sticks

12 THINKING GLOBALLY

Perhaps you have heard the expression, **"the world is flat."**

That is also the name of a book written by Thomas Friedman in 2005.

Friedman writes that technology is making it so easy for people all over the world to communicate and compete that no young adult can afford to think parochially ever again. Here is a snippet from Friedman's 500-page book:

"Globalization 3.0 (today) is shrinking the world from a size small to a size tiny and flattening the playing field at the same time. ... The dynamic force in Globalization 3.0 ... is the new found power for individuals to collaborate and compete globally...

Individuals must, and can, now ask, Where do I fit into the global competition and opportunities of the day, and how can I, on my own, collaborate with others globally?"

The point is actually quite simple.

If you want to succeed in your endeavor of choice you **MUST**:

(1) understand that you may be competing with people halfway around the world;

(2) understand how people of all ethnicities, cultures, and races think and communicate and;

(3) embrace diversity—learn from and grow with those who are not at all like you.

STEREOTYPES

A stereotype is a broad-strokes label put on people of certain races, cultures, religions, sexual orientations, or ethnicities. Stereotypes are impediments to communication and collaboration.

By now you know that everyone is different. This holds true for people of the same race, culture, and ethnicity. As soon as you try to typecast (stereotype) someone, you put a box around both you and them. You see the other people in a way that is most likely not accurate. And, you create a box around yourself because you create distrust and animosity in the other person.

If you are going to see in this FLAT WORLD of ours, you better kick stereotyping this minute. No two people are alike.

You must **embrace** the **differences** in people, the **diversity** in your school, your environment.

We don't learn by surrounding ourselves with people just like us.

Rather, we grow and evolve when we experience new people, places, and things. That is what diversity is all about.

Every single person you meet can help you. Maybe not right now but someday. They can teach you. How you see and experience the world is often very different from how others do. By embracing people of different races, cultures, and ethnicities; of different sexes, sexual orientations, and ages; of different physical and mental talents (and/or disabilities), you learn. **You learn a lot!**

One of the biggest mistakes people make is that they confuse the familiar with the universal. In other words, they presume that what is familiar—i.e., what is comfortable to them—is what is comfortable to lots of others (the universal). In making that mistake they often make significant errors of judgment, miss opportunities, and lose friendships.

GETTING INVOLVED

One great way to enrich yourself is to get involved in community activities— especially with people **NOT LIKE YOU**.

Have you ever worked in a soup kitchen? Do you presume that the people who eat there are very different from you? Maybe they are, maybe they're not. But, in any event, you can learn a lot from people who have been knocked around by life.

There are innumerable opportunities to learn from people different from you. Here are four suggestions:

1. Volunteer to work in a drug or alcohol dependency clinic.

2. Mentor a young adult of a different race than yours.

3. Work on a political campaign for a candidate you feel strongly about.

4. Give your time to a homeless shelter, a hospital, or other community organization.

In any of the above environments, you will encounter people experiencing life in a way that may be very different from what you are familiar with. **That is what growth is all about.**

13 FINANCIAL LITERACY

Wow, now we are getting into some **big topics**!

Money is one of those subjects that is very personal. How much do you have? How much do you make? How much do you want? Everyone will answer these questions differently in part because **money involves choices**.

What you make, what you spend, what you save, what you need—in each case the response to these questions will depend upon decisions you make during your life. Some people want as much money as they can possibly make and are prepared to sacrifice other aspects of their life to maximize their income. Other people do not want to center their lives on the acquisition of material items.

One author, T. Harv Eker (Secrets of the Millionaire Mind), speaks to your "financial blueprint: the information or 'programming' (about money) you received in the past and especially as a young child."

There is no right answer of course. **What matters is what matters to you.** For now, however, understand that money is a scarce commodity. That means it goes to those who provide economic value. In order to make a lot of money, you will need to prepare yourself to bring economic value to the business world. We will talk more about this.

THE BASICS OF FINANCE

In order to achieve the level of financial well-being you desire, you need to understand some basics of finance. There are, of course, a million things to learn. But let's start with five very basic principles:

1. It's not what you make that counts, it's what is left over after you spend what you make. It is your **net income** (after expenses and taxes) that we need to focus on.

2. If you do not track your income and expenses (and taxes), you will never get on top of your financial needs. You must make a **budget**—even if it's something rudimentary.

3. The government wants a portion of what you make. Get prepared to pay **lots** of income taxes over the course of your lifetime.

4. The government also wants you to contribute to your future financial well-being and health-care needs—in the form of **Social Security** and **Medicare**. Deductions for these amounts will come out of your paycheck.

5. **Debt** is the number-one way people get into a serious financial hole from which they cannot extract themselves. You need to be savvy about what you borrow and under what conditions.

BANKING

There are two purposes to a bank:

1. To help you save, invest, and administer your money—savings and checking accounts, Certificates of Deposit, debit cards.

2. To lend you money—car and home loans, credit cards.

Understanding your options when you walk into a bank is **critical**.

It is also important to understand that bankers are not your friend like your doctor or teacher. Bankers want to make money for their bank. And they want you to help them. So you need to realize that when you invest money in a bank product (e.g., a savings account), you are making the bank money. Ditto when you borrow money from a bank or use one of its loan products such as a credit card. **That is OK so long as the advantages to you of having or using that product are worth the costs.**

"A bank is a place where they lend you an umbrella in fair weather and ask for it back when it begins to rain!"

ROBERT FROST

BALANCING A CHECKBOOK

Balancing a checkbook is a basic component of budgeting.

The old joke,

**I CAN'T BE OUT OF MONEY,
I still have checks in my checkbook**

is … well, not funny.

Far too many people never get around to balancing their checkbook—essentially just keeping track of what they have in the account and what is going out with each check—and as a result get hit with lots of fees by their banker.

To balance your checkbook:

1. **Write down in your ledger every check you write and immediately total what you have left after that check.**

2. **Check your ledger against the monthly statement you receive from the bank.**

If you do not balance your checkbook, you are likely to get hit at some point with **"overdraft" fees**. These are fees banks charge you for writing checks that exceed the amount in your checkbook. **They are very expensive!** Wouldn't you rather spend time keeping your checkbook in balance than pay these fees?

A **debit card** allows you to access the money in your checking or savings accounts. Most debit cards have ATM capabilities so you can get cash when you need it. A debit card is safer than a credit card in that it is not a vehicle for borrowing money. If you try to use your debit card to purchase an item for more money than you have in your account(s), the purchase may get honored (with an overdraft fee) but at some point your banker will no longer honor these charges.

A **credit card** allows you to borrow money—to buy things with money you don't have. Every credit card has a credit line. For example, if you have a credit line of $500, you can borrow this amount from the bank just by using your card. If you exceed that amount there are fees. Then in a few weeks you will get a bill with a total of all that you owe the bank for the preceding weeks' charges. If you cannot pay the total, you will be charged interest on what you cannot pay. Interest rates on credit cards are quite high—the average rate today is about 15%.

"It is no accident that a credit card is so small and thin and easy to get out of your pocket or purse. If the credit card companies could oil the cards so that they slip out that much quicker, they would do that as well."

JIM RANDEL,
THE SKINNY ON CREDIT CARDS

BORROWING MONEY

Unfortunately, Shakespeare's advice does not work in the 21st century. At some point in your life, and probably sooner rather than later, you will be borrowing money (maybe even lending money). Perhaps you will have and use a credit card. Or, get a student loan ... or a car loan. Or borrow money from your family.

> "Neither a borrower nor a lender be;
> For loan oft loses both itself and friend.
> And borrowing dulls the edge of husbandry."
>
> WILLIAM SHAKESPEARE'S HAMLET
>
> (Polonius giving advice to his son Laertes as Laertes heads off to school.)

The fact is that borrowing money can be of great use to you if you do so **reasonably** and **responsibly**.

Borrowing allows you to purchase items before you have the ability to pay for them in full:

A college education,

a car,

necessities that you use your credit card to buy.

So long as you borrow with your eyes wide open (**don't kid yourself about your ability to repay the loan**) and with clarity as to the terms and conditions of repayment, then Shakespeare's warning should not apply to you.

UNDERSTANDING YOUR CREDIT SCORE

If you have ever used a credit card, you most likely have a credit score assigned to you. Here is how this works:

There are three major credit reporting companies:

Transunion,   Experian,   and   Equifax.

These companies are provided information about you from anyone who lends you money (e.g., banks) or has a financial relationship with you (e.g., landlords). These reporting companies compile this information into your credit report. By law they have to give you a copy of your report once a year. Go to **www.annualcreditreport.com.**

Credit scores range from a low of 300 to a high of 850. Your credit score is like a grade card. The scoring company (the biggest is Fair Isaacs Corporation) looks at your credit report and does some fancy mathematics to give you a score. This credit score presumably predicts how you will behave in the future when it comes to repaying lenders or other accounts with which you have an interest.

Your credit score is actually quite important because it is available to lots of people who will have an impact on your life: lenders, landlords, employers, and insurance companies.

One of your high priorities should be doing your best to keep your credit score up. **First rule:** pay your bills on time.

RENT, UTILITIES, AND LIFE'S ESSENTIALS

One of the hardest things to do is **"live within your means."**

In other words, keeping your consumption in line with your ability to pay for it. People get into debt problems when they make purchase decisions that are out of whack with their ability to pay for them. And it can all happen so quietly—little by little. Before you know it, big debt issues arise.

Every decision you make—which apartment to rent … how many people to live with … which cell phone service to use … where to shop for clothing and how much to spend … which purchases are essential and which can be put off for another time—must be made in light of your overall financial ability to earn and pay.

We all get impatient. **We all want what we want … WHEN we want it.** But, the key to staying out of financial trouble, out of serious debt, is to exercise patience and prudence in your purchase decisions. (How is that for some serious alliteration?)

"Patience, prudence and parsimony are the preferred purchasing priorities for people in college."

ANONYMOUS

(because no one would admit to having said this)

Before you consider a student loan, you should review all possible grants and scholarships that may be available to you. These, to be contrasted with loans, do not have to be paid back.

There are two main types of student loans: **government** (subsidized and unsubsidized) and **private** loans.

Private student loans come in many varieties. There is usually more flexibility in structuring a private loan than a subsidized loan. The largest private lender in the United States is a company called Sallie Mae.

Although **subsidized loans** require lots of paperwork and take more time to process, explore these loans in full before considering a private loan (or additional private lending). The interest rates on these loans are usually about half the amount of private loans. There is no requirement to make payments while you are in college. There are flexible repayment terms. There are, however, annual limits to what you can borrow—and a lifetime total as well.

IMPORTANT: Student loans are serious business. If you have financial trouble later in life and ever have to consider bankruptcy (a legal process for wiping out all your debts), one of the few debts that is not wiped out in bankruptcy is a student loan!

INCOME TAXES

Ouch! Sorry, but this subject just can't be avoided.

Like it or not, this is a subject about which you need to have a basic understanding.

The United States collects its income taxes in two ways:

1. **Income taxes are withheld from your paycheck by your employer.** This calculation is based on the number of exemptions you claim. When you get hired for a job you will fill out a Form 9, which tells the government how many exemptions you claim. For simplicity, think of an exemption as you and anyone else who is dependent on you for his or her care. The fact that the government withholds money from your pay does not mean you will have to pay that withheld amount in taxes. The withheld moneys often come back to you at the end of the year based on what you actually owe versus what was withheld from your income. The withholding is just to be sure you don't forget to pay your taxes.

2. **Every year U.S. citizens are required to pay by April 15th the taxes they owe the government for the preceding calendar year.** A tax return starts with Gross Income (everything you earned), minus your exemptions and deductions (for most students this is a set amount—what is called the standard deduction) to derive Taxable Income. A tax rate is then applied to your Taxable Income.

"Every year the government shoves you in a river with all your earnings in your pocket, whatever doesn't get wet you can keep."

WILL ROGERS

One of the lessons you can learn from senior citizens is that the decisions you make as a young adult will greatly impact your life in later years. How much you save. Your investment decisions. Debts or no debts.

That is why it is so **critical** that you use your college years to learn all you can about the financial world. You must **educate yourself** about the basics and not blindly take advice from anyone who has an agenda that may not be in your best interest.

Here is our **NUMBER ONE** rule for financial decisions.

If you do not fully understand a product, offering, or opportunity being proposed to you, **THEN PASS**—do not contribute your hard-earned dollars to something you do not totally comprehend.

Some people are dishonest and will suggest expenditures or investments that are just plain bad. Most people are honest but have to make a living and in doing so, don't always explain as carefully as they should all the plusses and minuses of various financial decisions.

"Use your time in college to boost your street smarts … learn everything you can about banking, income taxes, investments, debt and credit, insurance and career opportunities. The time you spend today—**to make yourself as financially savvy as possible**—will stand you in good stead as you bob and weave through the complicated financial world waiting for you outside your campus walls."

Jim Randel, The Skinny on Finance for the Young Adult

14 HEALTH

There are three types of health:

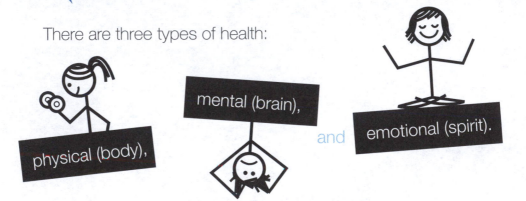

physical (body),

mental (brain),

and emotional (spirit).

College is a time of stress. Of too much to do with too little time to do it in. Of finding yourself. Of new experiences—some pleasant, some not. And then just when you start getting comfortable, college ends with a whole slew of new challenges—getting a job, making ends meet, crafting a future for yourself.

One of the most important pieces of advice available to you is that your enjoyment of college life, your ability to deal with competing stresses and pressures, your facility for "rolling with the punches," will be enhanced by the attention you pay to your health—mental, physical, and spiritual.

The pages that follow are about paying attention to **YOU**—making your health a priority and finding a balance between your needs and all that you need to do and be.

THE BASICS OF GOOD NUTRITION

For the most part, the path to good health is quite well marked:

1. Eat the right foods
2. Drink lots of fluids
3. Exercise
4. Get adequate rest

PIECE of cake! errr... **carrot cake** of course.

The challenge, of course, is finding the **time** and the **discipline** to do all the right things.

Let's start with nutrition. Here are **eight very important rules** of good nutrition:

1. Eat a good breakfast.

2. Eat five or six times during the day—rather than two or three huge meals.

3. Eat lots of vegetables.

4. Eat lots of fruit.

5. Drink lots of water.

6. Moderate your intake of white flours and sugars.

7. Don't eat right before going to bed.

8. Read labels—know what you are putting in your system.

That's it. If you are conscientious about those eight rules, you are on your way to a healthy body.

"A GOOD LAUGH AND A LONG SLEEP are the **best cures** in the doctor's book."

Irish proverb

"IF WE WERE MEANT TO POP OUT OF BED, we would sleep in **toasters**."

Anonymous

OK, you get it.

Sleep and rest are critical to rejuvenate your system. And for most, college is a time that challenges your need for sleep. Many students report feeling sleep-deprived **50% of the time.**

The fact is you can fool your body for short periods of time and function relatively well on less than six to eight hours of sleep per night. But, eventually your body's need for rest will catch up to you.

Note the "six to eight" hours of sleep. While most experts suggest eight hours, there are some people who function well on an hour or two less. But, anything under six hours a night is not considered healthy.

THE RIGHT EXERCISE PLAN FOR YOU

OK, now for some very exciting information. We have discovered the **Fountain of Youth** and we are going to tell you where it is. It is right outside your door!

Study after study after study have all established the benefits of exercise for longevity and good health. So, let's say you buy into the benefits of exercise. **What is the right plan for you?**

Well, experts would tell you that you should try to do something—anything that causes you to move—for about 30 minutes a day. That does not mean you need to visit the gym every day.

Any activity that causes you to work your body is good.

A brisk walk. A climb up the stairs instead of an elevator. Helping your friend move to a different dorm room. Whatever. **The point is to use that amazing body of yours.**

And for those of you who want to go the next level, physicians suggest four to five days a week of moderate to strenuous aerobic exercise. On some of those days, weight-training is also suggested. Five to six days in the gym should be enough, however. Almost everyone suggests one day off!

DRUGS & ALCOHOL

If there is a Fountain of Youth, there is also a Well of Abuse. Drugs can be just as devastating to human life as disease, accidents, and wars. Drugs and alcohol usually kill you slowly. The disease creeps up on you.

You know the facts.

You know the statistics on drug and alcohol use. So, if you want to experiment, that is your decision. But, **don't fool yourself. Drugs and alcohol are addictive.**

At least consider this one plea: **EVERYTHING IN MODERATION.** Drug and alcohol use to the extreme can kill you—and in some cases, not slowly. Every year there are stories of young adults who went too far—and who are no longer around to talk about it.

I'M OK, YOU'RE OK

"Most people are about as happy as they make up their minds to be."

ABRAHAM LINCOLN

One of the most important lessons a person learns over a lifetime is that there are few "normals." **We are all different.** We all have issues and history and pressures to deal with. And the best we can do—is the best we can do.

One stress we want to diffuse right now, however, is the worry that you are different from others—and thereby somehow less worthy or valued.

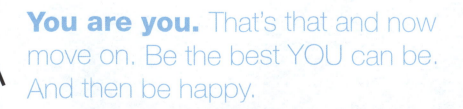

You are you. That's that and now move on. Be the best YOU can be. And then be happy.

HOW TO STICK TO YOUR PLAN

Once you decide on a plan that will enhance your health—whether it is eating better, exercising more, or staying away from drugs/alcohol—the trick (of course) is to **stick to the plan.**

Here are a few suggestions that may help you:

1. **Decide** in advance where you are likely to have problems.

2. **Figure out** exactly what you will do when you are in those challenging situations.

3. **Create** a mantra for yourself when you feel like you are losing the ability to stick with your plan. Repeat your mantra over and over.

4. **Plan** on slipping. We all slip at times. But, you can rebound by planning exactly what you will do after you slip—to get you back on track.

Oftentimes, the way to stick to a plan is to visualize and strategize all the situations where you may fall off your program. By doing that, you create responses that will help you stay the course.

WILL POWER AND SELF-DISCIPLINE

As it happens, Teddy Roosevelt knows a lot about self-discipline. Born very sickly (his mother remarked he looked like a "terrapin"), Teddy struggled with all sorts of illnesses during the first ten years of his life.

One day his father pulled him aside and said, "Teddy, you have the mind but without the body, you will never go as far as you might."

"The one quality which sets one apart from another—the key which lifts one to every aspiration while others are caught up in the mire of mediocrity—is not talent, formal education, nor intellectual brightness; it is self-discipline. With self-discipline, all things are possible. Without it, even the simplest goal can seem like the impossible dream."

TEDDY ROOSEVELT

It is reported that young Teddy said, "I will make my body." And he created an incredible physical regimen for himself, remaking his body and health along the way.

15 SELF-ASSESSMENT

You've been involved in **assessment** for your whole school life.

Every test you take is an assessment of how well you have mastered certain material. Every report card you got was an assessment of your performance as a student. Yet these are all someone else's assessment of you. Now that you have begun this new educational journey, more and more you need to be engaged in self-assessment.

You've read about critical thinking mostly in terms of all the new information that is coming at you in college. However, one of the most valuable areas on which to focus your critical-thinking skills is **yourself**. Self-awareness is a hallmark of a truly educated and mature person, because it is only when we are aware of who we are, our strengths and weaknesses, our hopes and dreams, the way we are perceived by others, our values and how true we stay to them, that we can make progress as students and as people.

Try this little exercise. ➔ Answer the question, **"Who am I?"**

Write down ten things that you are. Look at that list. Why did you choose the items that you did? Are they the most important things about you? The things that first came to mind? Do you want to make some changes? Go ahead. Now look at each item on your list and write down the things that you like about that quality.

1.

2.

3.

4.

5.

6.

7.

8.

9.

10.

For example, perhaps you wrote "reader" on the list. What you like about being a reader is that you know a lot about people, places, ideas, and history that you would never have discovered in "your own little world." Also, as a reader you have a rich source of entertainment that is easily accessible and keeps you thinking and happily absorbed.

Now that you are **more conscious** of what you like about being a reader, you will make more time for reading. If, however, there was little you could find to like about something on the list, you might try to remove that identity from your list and yourself.

Below is a list of twenty values and interests. Rate them from most important **(to you)** to least important.

This reflection is purely for your benefit, so be honest and thoughtful (see ACES, p. 44). Don't rate them the way you think you should, but according to what you **truly believe**.

1. Honesty	7. Health	14. Learning
2. Friendship	8. Safety	15. Individualism
3. Family	9. Kindness	16. Independence
4. Having fun	10. Laughter	17. Freedom
5. Love	11. Money	18. Politics
6. Service to others	12. Religion	19. Relaxation
	13. Work	20. Possessions

Did you have some difficult decisions? Were you surprised at some of the choices you made? A self-aware person is conscious of the values that underlie his or her actions.

Your values have an impact on everything you are and do. Your assessment of your goals, the way you spend your time, and the way you spend your money need to reflect the values you hold dear.

MISSION STATEMENT

Goals tell you where you want to go, but your **mission statement tells you where you want to end up**. Writing a mission statement gives you an opportunity to think about what you want your one and only life to mean now, when the choices you make will have such a huge impact on the person you will become.

Answers to these questions will help you create a **mission statement**:

- What do I want people to say about me when I'm gone?
- What makes me feel good about myself?
- What or who inspires me the most?
- What causes do I believe in or care about?
- If I could make a statement that would go out to the world, what would I say?

Your mission statement can be a series of statements such as:

I will contribute to society by giving time and money to charity organizations.

I will make use of my talents and abilities to create a good life for myself.

I will work hard and play hard.

Or your mission statement can say,

My mission in life is:

To be honest at all times.

To take care of my family.

To work hard to meet the challenges I encounter every day.

However you put it, just painting the big picture of what you want your life to mean should make clear to you what is most important to you.

Life provides a series of choices. You should be conscious of the **values**, **beliefs**, and **ideas** that guide the choices you make.

Self-assessment involves an honest appraisal of outcomes. This appraisal includes investigation into the reasons you got the results that you did.

Who is **in control** of your life? Hopefully your answer is **"I am."**

Let's test how much you actually believe that:

Are most things that happen to you the result of **your thoughts or actions?**

OR

Are most things that happen to you the result of **circumstances beyond your control?**

It's tempting to take credit for the good things, and to blame others for the bad. But the minute you see power over your life as residing outside of yourself you have become a **victim** rather than a **controller**.

When you see events happening because of actions you did or did not take, you know that you create your own outcomes. It's easy to accept that idea when it comes to getting an A on the test. Clearly, it's because you studied the right things for long enough, and used your best test-taking skills. But what if you did those things and got a bad grade on the test? Not your fault, right? It was your lousy teacher, or the fact that you are just not good at math.

Here is where seeing yourself as the controller makes a difference.

If you view a failing grade as confirmation that you are stupid and therefore shouldn't even try to succeed in the course, or that the teacher is a student-hating know-nothing, you probably will fail the course. Instead, turn your critical-thinking light on.

Analyze what happened, **clarify** your beliefs about causes to test the validity of them, and **evaluate** the possibilities of different ideas. See the relationships between the things you did or did not do, and the final outcome. **Different actions will change an outcome that you don't like.**

In the case of the failed test, what can you do so the next test will give you a different result? The possibilities are vast:

- Go to the tutoring center
- Form a study group
- Speak with the professor during office hours
- Work longer on your assignments so you are more prepared
- Study harder
- Review your test-taking skills

When you see the control over an outcome as residing in you rather than outside of you, **you have power over the outcome** rather than being a victim of circumstances.

When we take responsibility we change our actions, but it also helps to change our attitudes. We all have running sound tracks in our brains. You know, those times when you say to yourself,

"You idiot, of course Stephanie said she was busy when you asked if she wanted to study with you after class. She probably knows that you're stupid in math, and who could miss that huge pimple on your chin?"

That sound track is called **Self-Talk**. When self-talk is a constant negative stream (including calling ourselves names), it's almost impossible to improve outcomes that we don't like. When we see things in a new light, we can change our actions and results, or at least change the way we feel about what happens.

Using **positive self-talk**, after Stephanie's rejection, you might think:

"Stephanie is probably telling the truth about being busy. She rushed off—maybe she has another class. How could she know I'm stupid when the one time I answered a question in class I was right? And she's seen me without a pimple, so that one blemish isn't going to turn her off; in fact, I'm not a bad-looking guy. My mother told me so. I'll ask Stephanie if she wants to get together before class next week, maybe she'll have more time."

What's the **optimistic response** if Stephanie says no again?

"She's just one person who doesn't really know me. I'm sure there are other girls who will appreciate me; there have been in the past. I'll just take my time and get to know more people."

Part of self-assessment involves looking at your performance in the most positive way so that you can try again and do better in the future.

Many people, when asked why they don't do their assignments, study for tests, or even exercise on a regular basis, will answer that they are lazy.

What is laziness?

If you played a video game rather than revising your English essay, you were lazy, right? Yet if someone showed you a film of yourself playing your game, would you look like your idea of a lazy person? Or would you look active and involved?

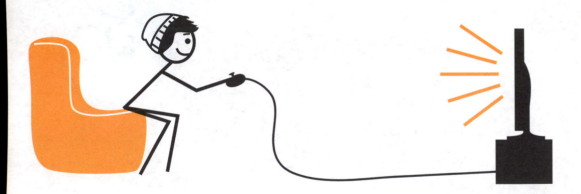

Maybe what we think of as laziness is simply about making choices.

When we choose the fun and easy thing that brings immediate satisfaction, rather than the more boring and difficult thing that won't pay off for a while, that's when we call ourselves lazy.

Some people seem to be able to make the hard choices easily. They do the extra math problems to better understand a challenging concept, instead of going to a party, because they are keenly aware that the pleasure of getting what they want in the long run (a good grade in math so they will be on the Dean's List) will be much greater than the pleasure of going to one party. They have **motivation**, the ability to move toward a desired goal.

When you engage in self-assessment, it is important to look at your level of motivation and determine **what is stopping you** from moving toward your goals.

Just a few obstacles you may face are:

- Your goals are not authentic (truly yours) or realistic

- You have no short-term goals that you can meet relatively quickly to give you an incentive to keep moving

- Your goals are not compelling—you don't want them enough to delay gratification of immediate satisfaction

- You fear failure

- You fear success

- You fear change

Once you have analyzed the obstacles to motivation, you can **make changes** in what you do or think to help you **move toward** the things that you want.

The opposite of movement is stagnation.

Success—we all want it whether it's in school, careers, or relationships.

As your first semester comes to a close, who can tell you whether you have been successful? You know the answer. Some assessments of your success are **tangible**:

- **Grades, honors, and awards**

- **Registration for next summer**

- **Meeting goals**

- **New friendships**

- **Familiarity with the services in your school that will help you**

- **Good relationships with faculty and staff**

- **Involvement with clubs, student activities, or service learning**

- **Healthy lifestyle**

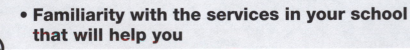

Some of the assessments of your success, however, are more **abstract**. They are the ones that point to your growth as a student, a person, and your ability not only to achieve success, but also sustain it over time:

- **Growth in a critical-thinking ability**

- **Growth in emotional intelligence, especially optimism**

- **Positive self-talk**

- **Goals that are compelling, measurable, and realistic**

- **A clearer understanding of your values and an effort to live by them**

- **A sense of your mission in life**

- **Responsibility**

- **Motivation**

What **grades** do you give yourself on all of the above items?

Find **accomplishments** to celebrate; there are always some.

Analyze your disappointments and **review** what you have learned about ways to get better results.

As long as you are **engaged** in the process of working on your success, you are on your way to **achieving** it.

NOTES

NOTES

NOTES

NOTES

NOTES